Go Free!

Robert M. Horn

InterVarsity Press
Downers Grove
Illinois 60515

InterVarsity Press is the book publishing
division of Inter-Varsity Christian Fellowship,
a student movement active on
campus at hundreds of universities,
colleges and schools of nursing.
For information about local and regional
activities, write IVCF, 233 Langdon St.,
Madison, WI 53703.

Quotations from the Old Testament are
from the Revised Standard Version
(copyrighted 1952 by the Division of Christian
Education, National Council of the Churches
of Christ in the United States of America).

Quotations from the New Testament are from
the New International Version
(copyrighted 1974 by The New York
Bible Society and published by Zondervan).

ISBN 0-87784-644-8
Library of Congress Catalog
Card Number: 76-4736

Printed in the United States of America

Contents

1 Relationships

We all have a sneaking sympathy with Charlie Brown's sentiment: 'I love mankind – it's people I can't stand.' People are the problem. Too often for comfort, relationships break down. The management locks out the workers who walk out. The parent resents the child who goes his own way. The husband argues with the wife who quarrels. Neighbours bear grudges and pass on gossip. Students in the same digs meet but never get through to each other.

Personal relationships matter. They mean more to us even than money, qualifications or success. If we are with those we love, we can put up with great hardships. We even enjoy the washing-up if the company is right! But the wrong company ruins the most beautiful occasions. The school-leaver or recent graduate may think that his first job is marvellous immediately after the interview; he may see it differently when he has to work under an irritable boss. How we get on with other people can make life or mar it.

Ourselves
Other people are problem enough, but we also have to live with ourselves. We co-habit with our conscience and our past, our failings and our misdeeds. We try to excuse ourselves, to plead extenuating circumstances or to switch off the voice of conscience – but without great success.

More seriously still, we have to come to terms with God. We may not like the thought, but this is the root problem of living. Sometimes people recognize this almost in spite of themselves. This happened recently in one university. The Christian Union held a book week, selling a particular title

7

from door to door in the student residences and also on four bookstalls round the campus. Along with the book they distributed a free hand-out in tabloid form, the contents of which were simply Paul's words in Romans (chapters 1 and 2) about the wrath of God and the nature and extent of human sin.

Student reaction was very definite. One girl came up to a bookstall and said accusingly, 'You're making us all feel guilty!' The Gay Society took sharp exception to Paul's plain speaking. Some of the Student Union committee tried to get the copies banned and the Christian Union ejected. The student newspaper published irate letters. Why were people so incensed? Why should a 1,900-year-old letter provoke them so much?

Christian Union members commented that it was not the 'Smile, Jesus loves you' approach that prompted these reactions. It was the truth about the basic relationship of God and man – the truths of wrath and sin and judgment. These truths, with which Paul began to open up the good news of Jesus Christ, were getting through to the minds and consciences even of those who professed to deny God. Certainly many of them seemed to know that they were answerable to Him.

Whether or not we react with such vehemence, the crucial issue for all of us is our broken relationship with God. What we are and do and want cuts us off from Him. This is the seed-bed of our other problems.

One-word answer

It is to this most basic problem that God supplies His most basic answer. In just one word the Bible marvellously sums up what God does about the problem – He 'justifies'. The word sounds a little strange today, though we do in fact sometimes use it in conversation. When we do (as, for example, in 'How can you justify that statement?' or 'I felt perfectly justified in taking the day off') it does not always have the precise meaning the Bible gives it. Yet it is a word worth grasping because it is so rich in meaning. It is a term so pre-

8

cisely chosen that attempts to find contemporary substitutes usually miss some of the original's significance.

Justification has to do first of all with the fractured personal relationship between God and ourselves. It tells us how that relationship may be restored. Of course, justification profoundly affects every other relationship; it enables us to understand and live with ourselves and others. But it begins by settling the fundamental matter of our standing with God. This is the theme of this book – the amazing grace of God in justifying sinners.

The need of understanding

When any relationship breaks down, the first requirement is that the parties in the conflict should come to understand each other. This applies in every sphere – between husbands and wives, parents and children, students and authorities, unions and management, police and public, government and electorate. And it applies in our relationship to God.

Obviously God understands us completely. No-one can hide anything from Him. The God we have to deal with sees everything and knows everything about us (see Heb. 4 :13). We cannot escape God's absolute knowledge of us : 'O Lord, thou hast searched me and known me ! . . . whither shall I flee from thy presence?' (Ps. 139 : 1, 7).

But we do not understand God, as many common ideas of Him demonstrate. Take as an example the truth that God is love. To many this is as natural and self-evident as gravity. 'Of course God is love,' they say. His love evokes no more surprise than the arrival of the daily paper. They ask questions only when the paper does not arrive – or when circumstances go wrong. 'What does the newsagent think he is doing?' 'What is a God of love doing, letting me suffer?' They assume that God is love. Just as they expect student grants or old-age pensions from the state, so they expect love from God. The heavenly welfare state, they argue, ought at least to match the earthly.

No attitude could be further from the truth. God *is* love, but the Bible never puts in the 'of course' when it talks of His love. Rather, its writers always catch their breath in amazement, in an ecstasy of total wonder. 'The steadfast love of the Lord *never ceases*, . . . his mercies never come to an end; they are new *every morning*' (La. 3 :22, 23). Paul's pulse-rate seems to quicken when he recalls that 'the Son of God . . . loved *me* and gave himself for *me*' (Gal. 2 :20). God's love is always supernatural, always a miracle, always the last thing we deserve.

When the Bible looks at those whom God loves, it can find no explanation in them for His love – no attractiveness, no special qualities, nothing that can draw out His love. For example, the Israelites were told that 'it was not because you were more in number than any other people that the Lord set his love upon you and chose you' (Dt. 7 :7). God does not love His people because they are worthy or lovable. The explanation given to the Israelites is still the only one : the Lord loves you 'because the Lord loves you' (verse 8). God loves because He loves. That may sound like mere repetition, but in fact it is staggering. The source and the reason for His love are in Him, not in us. We cannot account for His love in terms of any outside stimulus.

No compulsion
God does not have to love us or justify us. He is under no constraint of any kind. We can put pressure on our family or friends to 'love' us; we cannot force God to take us in, for God is quite different. We cannot measure Him by our standards. He is above and beyond them. This is part of what the Bible means by speaking of God as holy. He is someone 'other', set apart, not one of us. He is over against us and His love comes out of His otherness.

God was love before ever He made man. There was love eternally between Father, Son and Spirit. This is why God *alone* is love. Of course, there are deeds and attitudes which are loving – a couple's love for each other or a mother's love for her child, for example. But apart from God there is no absolutely pure love in the world. Human love is always mixed with other motives : we love for what we get in return, or for the pleasure it gives, or for the feeling of having done the right thing. We love because we are attracted or because we need love. But God's love is unique. He loved us first, before ever we had made any move towards Him. 1 John 4:19 actually says that 'we love because he first loved us'. That is, our whole capacity to know and give love comes through His prior love for us.

This is why it is wrong to say 'love is God' – a statement the Bible never makes. That gets things the wrong way round, because it starts with *our* view of love and then says 'God is that'. It reduces God's love to the limits of our understanding. Such thinking can never be right. Compared with human love even at its highest, God's love is 'another' love, a holy love. So we must understand what God's love means and reject false ideas of it.

Understanding God's wrath

It is equally important to understand God's wrath and judgment. These terms are naturally offensive to us for at least two reasons. First, they seem medieval and barbaric. They seem to belong to the age when people believed in retribution. Today, it is said, we know better. In our law-courts, for example, we do not operate on such outmoded principles as punishment. We emphasize rehabilitation, retraining, reform and treatment. Surely, say some, God is not behind the times? Secondly, many people think that these are just Old Testament ideas, which Christ has now made obsolete.

We cannot, however, dismiss these notions so easily. The facts of absolute right and wrong and of justice and guilt linger in our consciences long after progressive thinkers have denied them. They correspond to something basic in the moral make-up God has given us. And no less a person than the compassionate Son of God attests the fact of divine wrath. Indeed it is Christ who teaches it most clearly. From the same lips on the same occasion came two statements. One was a gracious invitation ('Come to me . . . and I will give you rest'); the other spoke of a *worse* judgment for His hearers than befell Sodom (Mt. 11:24–30).

Totally different

As we read the Bible we find that God's wrath, like His love, is pure and holy, quite different from ours. It is part of His otherness, for there is purity behind His anger. His eyes are too pure to look on evil; He cannot contemplate wrong with pleasure (see Hab. 1 :13). What is more, God's purity is too intense to ignore evil. He cannot pretend that it is not there or does not matter. His justice is too true to let sin go un-checked and unpunished. His love of all that is honourable, just, pure, lovely, gracious, excellent – that love is too abso-lute for Him to pass over what corrupts and destroys.

To us, sin is the fault of circumstances, or indeed of God Himself. We follow the first-ever excuse for sin : 'The woman whom thou gavest to be with me. (Yes, it's all your fault, God), she gave me fruit' (Gn. 3 :12). We try to turn down the volume when the truth of God's wrath begins to get through to us. We do not like to receive it loud and clear. Yet God remains 'a righteous judge, and a God who has indignation every day' (Ps. 7 :11). God is against sin, against all sin, always against sin. He can never tolerate or overlook it. This is why Paul's account of the good news begins by affirming that 'the wrath of God is being revealed from heaven against all the godlessness and wickedness of men' (Rom. 1 :18). This God of wrath is the God and Father of the Lord Jesus Christ, the One whom Christ addressed as 'Righteous Father' (Jn. 17 :25). God is above all holy – Father, Son and Spirit.

From start to finish the Bible advertises God's holiness. Everything He does is holy and perfect. He may not always act in kindness or always in wrath, but He invariably acts in holiness. He can never bypass the moral law in which He expresses His holiness. To do so would be to deny Himself. Creation expressed His holy perfection :'And God saw every-thing that he had made, and behold, it was very good', with-out blemish or sin (Gn. 1 :31). His holiness shines out in the Ten Commandments, which were no stop-gap expedient to keep rebellious nomads in check, but which express His eternal nature. What He requires from men springs from what He is in Himself. Supremely, He displayed His purity in His Son, 'one who is holy, blameless, pure, set apart from sinners' (Heb. 7 :26). This holiness will be demonstrated in the last judgment: 'Shall not the Judge of all the earth do right?' (Gn. 18 :25).

Not a fit of temper

It is because God is holy that His standards are absolute and His wrath a reality. To us wrath is an emotive word, but God's wrath has none of the sinful associations that attach to human wrath. With Him wrath does not mean a fit of temper or an emotional outburst. Our wrath is like that because we are touchy and proud. Anger possesses us and gets out of control so that we regret it later. It always springs from mixed motives. But God's anger is not like that. It is pure, just and good, His righteous attitude to all evil and the mirror-image of His love of all that is good. God's wrath is His fixed hatred of sin and His determination to act accordingly. Therefore 'it is a dreadful thing to fall into the hands of the living God' (Heb. 10 :31). As Christ said, the unbelieving and disobedient will 'go away to eternal punishment' (Mt. 25 :46). He was forthright when He described the final state of those under God's wrath as being 'in torment . . . in agony in this fire' and with 'a great chasm' fixed between the justified and the condemned (see Lk. 16 :19–31). Such terms underline the gravity of the wrath of the Lamb (Rev. 6 :16).

Real now

God's wrath will be finally displayed in the judgment, but it is also a present reality. This is what Paul wrote in Romans 1. Man has a knowledge of God, but suppresses it. He does not want to know. He claims to be wise and, instead, becomes a fool. And God, acting judicially, hands him over to the consequences of his own folly. He gives him up to the lusts of his nature, to dishonourable passions, to evil inventiveness. Such people not only put evil into practice themselves; they end up with their moral awareness so distorted that they actively applaud those who do evil.

It may be unwise to be too specific in applying Romans 1 today (though that university example shows that the chapter still speaks to our situation). Yet many features of Western culture are identical with those which Paul says result from God's wrath. Many people, not least those who have good claim to human wisdom, reject God. They trust their own knowledge, skills and technology. They attack God's arrangements for human life, especially in relation to the family. They blur God's distinctions between right and wrong, liberty and licence, male and female. They disregard God's commands and approve evil. One quotation from a book on the family illustrates this : 'Making love is good in itself and the more it happens in any way possible or conceivable between as many people as possible more and more of the time, so much the better.'[1] When men reject God, sooner or later they reject everything He has ordained. The same book is against all 'familial structures' : 'we have to paralyse the functioning of each family, school, university, factory, business corporation, television company, film-industry segment.'[2] All must go because God's order for human living is thrown overboard. The state of society commended by such a writer is not far from what Paul describes as the result of God's 'handing men over'. God's wrath is not to be pushed vaguely into the future. He is against sin now also and will make this plain in His dealings with men.

This is the God we face – the God of holy love and holy wrath, who loves righteousness and hates evil. We need to see the character of the God from whom we are estranged if ever we are to be reconciled. Talk of reconciliation must begin here with the realities of God, rather than with talk of 'come and be happy in Jesus'. We must take seriously God's god-ness, His otherness.

Some conclusions ruled out
These truths bring us to certain negative conclusions, for they rule out some ideas of how God accepts us.

1. It is impossible for God simply to pronounce us pardoned. He cannot just say 'let bygones be bygones'. That would be God saying that sin does not matter. That would be God condoning all our past rebellion. But sin is no light

[1] David Cooper, *Death of the Family* (Penguin, 1971), pp. 47f.
[2] *Ibid.*, p. 123.

matter; it is of infinite consequence because it is against the infinite, holy God.

2. It is not enough for God just to give us the example of Christ. No example can remove our past guilt, give power over sin in our present experience or assure our future destiny. We *ought* to follow His example, but we cannot. Failure to follow it only condemns us.

3. A change in our attitude is not enough on its own. Some approaches try to make the story of the prodigal son into the whole gospel. If we are sorry, they say, the Father will run to embrace us while we are still at a distance. Now clearly we must repent, but that in itself does not cancel our sin.

We must understand what God has revealed about Himself. He cannot accept us unless something is done about our sin. Sin brings guilt and guilt requires punishment; only when that punishment is borne can we experience forgiveness of sins.

Understanding ourselves

We must also understand ourselves. God calls us sinners – but what is sin? It is easy to see what 'sins' are; the Bible describes them in many ways – failures, errors, trespassings, going astray, missing the target. They are also anti-social and may become crimes. But basically even anti-social sins are offences against God, not just against others. They are hateful, and bring moral contamination and spiritual death. It is not hard to press the definition further to include motives. Even if the desire to kill, abuse or deceive is not carried out, it is still a sin.

We are not, however, merely guilty of sins, serious though they are. There is more to our condition than that. We can put it this way : I am not a sinner because I commit sins; rather, I commit sins because I am a sinner. The essence of sin is in what I am – a rebel against God. Sin is deliberate disobedience to God, the refusal to love God with all our being. Sin is 'me first' in defiance of God. We are not guilty of all the sins. We may even be like Paul, 'as for legalistic righteousness, faultless' (Phil. 3 :6). But we are all guilty of

15

sin. 'False and full of sin I am' wrote Charles Wesley.[3] He did not mean he had broken every rule in the book; rather, he was without love for God, saturated with self-love. That is sin.

Sin makes us guilty. It does not merely bring guilt-feelings, but actually incurs guilt, which shuts us out of God's presence, whether we feel the force of that or not. Sooner or later it also brings guilt-feelings: the sense of shame, the knowledge that we cannot look God in the eye, the fear of Him turning His searching gaze on us.

People with a record

We are, in police terms, men and women with a record of actual sins. And we are hardened in our attitude of rebellion against God. We are culpable on both counts and, in addition, powerless. In its wrestling with us, sin has extracted a submission; left to ourselves, we have lost not merely a few rounds but the over-all contest. Sin pins us down and we are without strength (Rom. 5:6), unable to please God (Rom. 8:8). We do not struggle with sin on equal terms with a 50-50 chance, but are its utter slaves, as Christ, who knows what is in man, said (Jn. 8:34).

This seems a harsh picture if we compare ourselves with others. But the Bible contrasts us as sinners both with man as God made him and with Christ, God-become-man. God created man upright, noble, capable, gifted and good. Sin has not fully erased the marks of man-the-image-of-God; but the marks that are still discernible show only how far man has fallen. This seems a harsh view in another way: it appears to overlook all the good that people still do. No-one denies that people do many deeds which are good in themselves; yet one distinction must be remembered. What is good in itself may not be good before God. Take an illustration from the days of pirate ships. Crew members could work hard for each other, be honest among themselves and helpful to others in the ship's company. All such actions were good. Their kindness actually was kindness. But their actions

[3] From the hymn 'Jesu, Lover of my soul' by Charles Wesley (1707–88).

were also wrong. Why? Because they served to keep the ship a pirate ship in violation of law. For one thing, their good deeds were highly selective; they did not help all in need. Even the good deeds grew out of their rebellion, expressing and reinforcing it.[4] It is the same with us. Our good deeds lack the one thing which would make them acceptable to God, for they spring from rebellious hearts.

No leverage with God

These unpalatable truths about ourselves bring us to certain conclusions about our relationship with God, and chiefly that we cannot earn acceptance with Him. We can do nothing even to catch His eye. We cannot spruce up our character so that God will come over to us. It is impossible for us to strike a bargain with Him : 'God, if you will take me in, I'll give my life to you.' To bargain we must be in a bargaining position; that means we must be able to bring some pressure to bear. In industrial relations both unions and management have some leverage with each other. Unions can call men out; management can fire them. But in our situation before God we have no leverage whatsoever. We cannot do one little thing to put ourselves in the right with Him. That sounds fatally depressing, and it is. By showing us the truth about ourselves God brings us to despair of all do-it-yourself religion. Only when we come to an end of self-help will we begin to look for God's help. Then we begin to discover that He can do what we cannot. Through justification He deals with our sin and brings us into the relationship for which we were created.

But what exactly is this justification which promises hope to the condemned?

[4] This illustration is adapted from Loraine Boettner, *The Reformed Doctrine of Predestination* (Eerdmans, 1932; reissued 1960), pp. 69f. Boettner himself takes it from W. D. Smith, *What is Calvinism?*

2 God's prerogative

I cannot forgive someone who wrongs you and you cannot forgive a person who hurts me. Only the individual who is wronged has the power to forgive. This is true also with God : He alone can pardon the guilt we incur by sinning against Him. Only God can clear the guilty.

From the time of Abraham this truth stands out in the Bible. It was God who justified him, as it is always God who justifies the ungodly (Gn. 15 :6; Rom. 4 :5). So the great concern of anyone with spiritual awareness is, according to the Bible, 'how can a man be just before *God*?' (Jb. 9 :2).

The psalmist knew this. He hardly dared plead for forgiveness, for he knew the total holiness of God. He could only acknowledge with fear : 'If thou, O Lord, shouldst mark iniquities, Lord, who could stand?' (Ps. 130 :3). If God were to produce his sins in evidence against him, his cause would be lost; but, amazingly, 'there is forgiveness with thee' (verse 4). And with no-one else. 'To the Lord our God belong mercy and forgiveness' (Dn. 9 :9).

Jesus brought this home in His parable about the proud, self-reliant Pharisee and the penitent tax-collector. The Pharisee overlooked the fact that God alone could justify. 'Lord,' he said, 'if you are going to hold people's sins against them, that's all right by me. That tax-collector over there doesn't stand a chance, of course. But I'm fine' (see Lk. 18 :9–14). He thought he could justify himself; and he was wrong. Justifying is God's prerogative, always and exclusively.

Justification means something God does. Indeed, it means a very specific thing God does. It is true that the God who

18

justifies also gives new life (regeneration), prompts spiritual growth (sanctification) and will one day make us perfect (glorification). Some run all these together and say that all He does is 'one divine act'.[1] But this just spreads confusion. It steals away our true understanding and enjoyment of what God has done. The Bible does not equate these terms. It says that the *one* God does all these related things; they are all parts of His one plan, but one part is not the whole or to be confused with another. Justification has a distinct meaning.

What does justification mean?

We still talk about 'justifying a statement'. We do not mean that we alter it to *make* it just – a statement either is just or it is not. All we can do is to win a verdict for it and get it accepted. That is not too far from the Bible's meaning.

The idea comes in the Bible before the actual word. Abraham, we are told, 'believed the Lord; and he reckoned it to him as righteousness' (Gn. 15:6; Rom. 4:3). Notice what this says. It does not say that justification instantly made Abraham righteous inwardly; in fact, Genesis goes on to show many of his subsequent sins. But God reckoned righteousness to his account. Paul used this word 'reckon' or 'impute' in writing to one of his friends. Philemon's slave, Onesimus, had wronged him, but had later been converted. So Paul wrote to Philemon : 'If Onesimus has done you any wrong or owes you anything, charge (reckon) it to me' (Phm. 18). Paul had the debt transferred to himself, and so Onesimus was cleared of the charges and welcomed back.

In a similar way God cleared Abraham of all the charges against him. Like all of us, he was a spiritual bankrupt. He could not work his way into spiritual solvency, but God did two things. Negatively, He did not reckon Abraham's sin against him; He did not enter it in his debit column. Positively, He reckoned His own divine righteousness to Abraham and entered that to Abraham's credit. So God justified Abraham.

The Bible gives us several *words* to help us understand

[1] Hans Küng, *Justification: the doctrine of Karl Barth and a Catholic reflection* (Burns and Oates, 1964), p. 68.

this truth. To reckon or impute righteousness is one of the synonyms for justify. There are others – not counting sins against us, covering sins, or crediting righteousness to us (Rom. 4:6–8). And of course there are the words for justification in both Testaments. The two nouns for justification occur between them just three times in the New Testament, but the verb comes in thirty-seven places. In addition the Bible gives us illustrations of this truth – and in those that follow, these words (and, where relevant, their opposites) are in italics.

Verdict of 'not guilty'

Joseph was sold by his brothers into Egypt as a slave. When later he was Chancellor in Egypt during the famine, his brothers came down for supplies. Joseph gave them food, but had his own silver cup hidden in the top of Benjamin's sack. This was only 'discovered' when Joseph's steward followed the brothers as they left. Naturally they were in a panic: 'What shall we speak? Or how can we *clear ourselves*? God has found out the guilt of your servants' (Gn. 44:16). They wanted a verdict of 'not guilty' before Joseph.

In the civil arrangements for Israel, one of God's provisions was this: 'If there is a dispute between men, and they come into court . . . the judges decide between them, *acquitting* the innocent and *condemning* the guilty' (Dt. 25:1).

As Solomon stood before the people to dedicate the Temple, part of his prayer was: 'If a man sins against his neighbour . . . then hear thou in heaven, and act, and judge thy servants, *condemning* the guilty . . . and *vindicating* the righteous' (1 Ki. 8:31, 32).

God Himself speaks in these legal terms: 'I will not *acquit* the wicked' (Ex. 23:7). Isaiah uses the terms of a law-court to speak of the coming of the great Servant of the Lord. There Christ says: 'He who *vindicates* me is near. Who will contend with me? Let us stand up together (as in court). Who is my adversary? Let him come near to me. Behold, the Lord God helps me; who will *declare me guilty*?' (see

Is. 50:7–9). Paul takes up that theme for the comfort of Christians: 'Who will *bring any charge* against those whom God has chosen? It is God who *justifies*. Who is he that *condemns*?' (Rom. 8:33, 34).

To justify is the opposite of to condemn.

A judge's verdict

It is a judge who condemns and a judge who acquits. The background is that of the law-courts. There the accusations are made and the judge sits to give a verdict. That verdict must be just, for the Bible is hot against those who 'acquit the guilty for a bribe' (Is. 5:23). (Incidentally a good judge will also be concerned for the reform and rehabilitation of a condemned man; but justice must be done first. Only on that basis can true help be given, for it is only in that way that the individual is treated with dignity as a responsible person and not just another case for treatment.[2])

Isaiah pictures the whole world of sinners assembled in God's court. 'Let us together draw near for judgment,' says God; 'the Lord has taken his place to contend, he stands to judge his people' (Is. 41:1; 3:13). The charges are brought, by conscience and the devil as well as by God. The great question is: what verdict will the Judge of all the earth pronounce? Condemned? or justified?

Acquitted and welcomed

When God justifies it means more than bare acquittal. 'We need the voice which says, not merely, "you may go; you are let off your penalty"; but "you may come; you are welcomed into my love".'[3] Justification deals with past, present and future – with all our sins for the duration of eternity.

1. It includes pardon and forgiveness, for God remits and so covers *the past*. It means our account is settled. God cancels our debt and puts His righteousness down to our name.

[2] *Cf.* C. S. Lewis, *The Humanitarian Theory of Punishment* (Marcham Manor Press).
[3] H. C. G. Moule, *Justification by Faith* (1903; reissued Falcon Press, 1959), p. 5.

We have no past record to answer for when God has justified. 'The past cannot be reversed except by accounting it reversed.'[4] And that God does.

2. Justification refers to *the present*, for it gives access to God and leads on to adoption into God's family (Gal. 4 :5, 6). God gives us His authority to call ourselves His children now (Jn. 1 :12; 1 Jn. 3 :2). God constitutes us righteous in Christ (Rom. 5 :19).

3. It also refers to *the future*. It assures us that, when all our life is exposed at the day of judgment, God's verdict of 'justified' will still stand. It gives us immunity at the bar of God because of Christ. It promises that, having been made joint-heirs with Him, we shall then inherit the full riches of glory (Rom. 8 :17).

This is all because justification relates us to the righteousness of God. This is actually the point at which Paul begins to open up the great treatment of justification in Romans. He is proud of the gospel : it is God's power for salvation for one specific reason, that in it 'a righteousness from God is revealed' (Rom. 1 :17).

Luther's troubled conscience

Martin Luther tells us how he came to see the true significance of this phrase from Romans chapter 1.

'I greatly longed to understand Paul's Epistle to the Romans and nothing stood in my way but that one expression, "the justice (righteousness) of God", because I took it to mean that justice whereby God is just and deals justly in punishing the unjust. My situation was that, although an impeccable monk, I stood before God as a sinner troubled in conscience, and I had no confidence that my merit would assuage him. Therefore I did not love a just and angry God, but rather hated and murmured against him. Yet I clung to the dear Paul and had a great yearning to know what he meant.

'Night and day I pondered until I saw the connection between the justice of God and the statement that "the just shall live by his faith". Then I grasped that the justice of God

[4] J. H. Newman, *Lectures on Justification* (2nd edition, 1840), p. 73.

is that righteousness by which through grace and sheer mercy God justifies us through faith. Thereupon I felt myself to be reborn and to have gone through open doors into paradise. The whole of Scripture took on a new meaning, and whereas before "the justice of God" had filled me with hate, now it became to me inexpressibly sweet in greater love. This passage of Paul became to me a gate of heaven. . . .'[5]

In the gospel the righteousness of God does not mean He pronounces judgment *against* sinners, but that He provides righteousness *for* them. By imputing Christ's righteousness to them, He declares them free from all the demands of the law.

A change of status

So justification is a matter of a verdict and a status. Now God is also concerned to change people, for He wants them to be different. He calls the justified to become like Christ. His Spirit lives in them to lead them to holiness. Those He adopts are to develop the family likeness. But He begins by changing their status.

This view of our relation to God is the exact opposite of the way we naturally think. If we take God seriously at all, we tend to think we must make ourselves righteous rather than have God declare us pardoned. Now God's way is to deal with our guilt and our status and *then* to deal with our heart and will and character. Yet we imagine that if our character is changed, then our status will be assured. If there is some improvement *in* us, then God will declare Himself *for* us.

This idea lies behind a popular misconception of justification – that it is not to declare but to make us righteous : not to impute, but to impart righteousness. According to this view what settles justification is not God's verdict as judge but my inward state of holiness. What God does is to infuse or inject His righteousness into me. Justification is not what He does objectively for me, but what He produces subjectively in me.

[5] Cited in R. H. Bainton, *Here I Stand: Martin Luther* (Hodder and Stoughton, 1951; reissued Mentor Books, 1955), pp. 50f.

This error – for that, as we shall see, is what it is – has vital practical consequences. Many people wonder whether they are good enough for God; perhaps you do. You think of your failures, your guilty silence in witness, your dubious motives even in prayer, and you are tempted to think you must have ruled yourself out of God's favour. You are just not good enough, and you know that you cannot atone for your past. Now if justification means that God *makes* righteous, then you know how to test your standing. You must find evidence that you are righteous 'really and truly, outwardly and inwardly, wholly and completely'.[6] According to such teaching, if you are like that, you are justified. If that is lacking, you are not. Your justification depends absolutely on you and on whether you are holy. The holiest person is the most justified.

So, on this view, our justification can grow. 'The justified increase in the very justice they have received . . . and are justified the more.'[7] But it can also decrease. 'Those who are declining in their obedience . . . are diminishing their justification.'[8] What is worse, our justification can be lost. Some 'have received the grace of justification but have lost it through sin'.[9] It is not just that *assurance* of justification wanes; justification itself can disappear. Thus our justification depends on us. We may have the church or the sacraments or the Spirit to help, but in the last analysis it depends on us. We must justify, or re-justify, ourselves. We must, for example, 'make the effort to regain through the sacrament of penance and by the merit of Christ the grace (we) have lost'.[1]

[6] Hans Küng, *op. cit.*, pp. 203f.
[7] Decrees of the Council of Trent (1546–63), chapter 10; from the Council's sixth session, 1546–7. Cited, *e.g.*, in J. F. Clarkson, J. H. Edwards, W. J. Kelly and J. J. Welch (eds.), *The Church Teaches: Documents of the Church in English Translation* (B. Herder Book Co., Missouri, 1955), p. 236.
[8] J. H. Newman, *op. cit.*, p. 169.
[9] Council of Trent, chapter 14; *op. cit.*, p. 239.
[1] *Ibid.*

Trying to make it

This is precisely what Paul and Luther tried to do – to make themselves so holy that God would accept them. Both came to see the black despair of that way, for such teaching has a sad effect on individuals. Someone influenced by it put his position to me like this : 'Justification is like a circle of grace round God. I entered the circle when I was baptized. I stay in it as long as I believe. If I sin grievously, I withdraw myself from it and must re-enter by penitence and faith. Should I die when I am outside the circle, I am lost.' What a pitiful existence! The only joy he had from his religion was when he could get away from it. Apart from the error of it, that way made him so terribly self-centred. His whole thought was, 'I must keep *myself* in the circle. *I* must try harder. I must improve *myself*. *I* must make it.' His life's concern was whether he could achieve his own justification.

This is what is at stake here; it is no exaggeration to say that the whole Christian life hinges on whether 'justify' means 'make righteous'. Because this is so crucial, I want briefly to look at the arguments for and against.

Does it make us righteous?

What are the arguments for taking it as 'making righteous'? They run like this. If God reckons a sinner righteous when he is still *un*righteous, then God is just playing with words. If His objective declaration does not alter my subjective condition, His words do not correspond to reality. To treat me *as if* I were holy (when patently I am not) is a deception. The 'as if' makes it derisory.

We must take this view seriously. Many feel its force in their own conscience whenever they are tempted to think, 'How can I claim to be worthy of God's love?' So, the argument runs, we must avoid the fiction of an empty declaration from God. It is no use having God say something which does not happen. So we must stress the power of God's word and assert that what God's word says happens, because His word brings it into being. Christ's mere word raised Lazarus. He did not say 'Come out' only to leave him in the tomb; divine power was in Christ's word. And so it is when God declares justice to a sinner. 'He declares a fact, and makes it a fact by declaring it.'[2] Unlike the word of man, God's word *does* what it speaks. God says, 'That man is just'; and he is. 'His sins are forgiven, and man is just in his heart.'[3]

This argument may be rather loosely linked to Scripture, but it has its own inner logic. Moreover, it seems to support the truthfulness and power of God. It is attractive to many because they dislike any talk of sacrifice, atonement or substitution. They want religion to be a matter of man's subjective commitment, not God's objective standards. They emphasize what happens *in man* and anything that avoids depending totally on God has an obvious appeal.[4] This appeal has always been felt in Roman Catholic circles – and still is (see Appendix 2 on page 125). But this view appeals to many who would never dream of calling themselves Roman Catholics. It will always be with us, not because Roman Catholicism has taught it, but because it expresses the reaction of the rebel heart to the idea of depending wholly on God.

Two questions

Clearly this view is right when it says that God's word is sovereign; that cannot be questioned. But two other questions may be put.

1. Does Scripture show that the justified are righteous in themselves? Clearly not. Remember the faults of Old Testament believers – Abraham, Moses, David, Elijah. Think of the alarming life of some New Testament believers; those at Corinth were behaving 'like mere men' (1 Cor. 3 :3). The apostle Peter fell, not only in denying Christ but later in pulling out of fellowship with Gentile believers to ingratiate himself with Jewish Christians. No believer is perfect until he sees Christ in glory (1 Jn. 3 :2). This is precisely why the Bible makes provision for believers who fall : 'if we confess

[2] J. H. Newman, *op. cit.*, p. 87.
[3] Hans Küng, *op. cit.*, p. 204.
[4] *Cf*. Hans Küng, *op. cit.*, p. 269. 'What is especially significant, however, is that the greater number of leading contemporary Protestant theologians have given up the purely extrinsic declaration of justice.'

our sins, he is faithful and just and will forgive us our sins' (1 Jn. 1:9). 'If anybody does sin, we have one who speaks to the Father in our defence' (1 Jn. 2:1). So the 'making righteous' dogma does not correspond with either the teaching of Scripture or the facts of experience.

2. What precisely does God declare when He justifies? Not that the sinner is now inwardly just. The words never mean that. This is shown, for example, in Luke 7:29: 'all the people . . . acknowledged that God's way was right', or 'justified God'. People did not and could not make God righteous. They could only recognize or declare it. And what God declares is that the believing sinner is forgiven, acquitted, accepted (Rom. 5:1; 8:1; Acts 13:38, 39). God declares him to be in His family, adopted and welcomed (Gal. 4:5; Rom. 5:2). God asserts that no charges will be brought against him (Rom. 8:33) and that His wrath no longer rests on him. *All* that God so declares happens. That individual is genuinely and for eternity an adopted child of God. That is no fiction. There is no make-believe about it. It is genuine, spiritual fact. No adopted child always shares his new parents' outlook and ways, but that does not make the adoption a fiction. Nor is divine adoption a fiction simply because the believer still has sin in him. Rather it is out of the new status and grace he has been given that his new life grows. (It is not accidental that adoption figures so little in Roman Catholic teaching; the two are not compatible.) God declares His believing children to be brought out of the condemned cell and into the irreversible welcome of heaven. He declares them to be livingly united to Christ.

No legal fiction

This is the meaning of justification. The 'making just' theory dissolves all hope before God by making salvation depend on us. It rules out assurance and so denies all the Bible truths about the blessings of the children of God. Those blessings are closed to all who trust their own intrinsic righteousness. It is God who justifies, not we who can fit ourselves for heaven. It is God's verdict, not our achievement. 'Ransomed, healed, restored, forgiven' – that is what God says

27

and that is what is. There is no legal fiction or make-believe. But there is this question : how can this *righteous* God declare *sinners* accepted? In our terms that sounds like justifying an untrue statement. On what basis therefore can He justify without becoming party to sin? That is the real question.

3 Lowered standards?

To anyone who takes God seriously it is a real problem to know *how* He can justify sinners. Indeed it was a problem to God.

He had no such problem with creation. He had only to say 'Let there be' and there was. Christ had no problem with the wind and waves. He had merely to say 'Peace' and the storm was gone. The Spirit has no problem with sinners. His voice speaks life into the dead. But justification is a problem to God in this sense – it involves more than simply His sovereign power. He cannot merely say to sinners 'Come on in'. If He received us just like that, He would be condoning our sin, for He is holy and we are not. Strictly it should be a case of 'never the twain shall meet'. 'Nothing impure will ever enter (heaven), nor will anyone who does what is shameful or deceitful' (Rev. 21 :27).

We read of God accepting successive generations of believers from Abraham onwards, but with nothing permanently satisfactory done about their sin. God passed over their faults (see Rom. 3 :25), and in so doing seemed to soil His hands. This is the problem, and the whole Old Testament magnifies it. Similarly the father welcomed the prodigal. And it was said of Christ that 'this man welcomes sinners' (Lk. 15 :2). It looks therefore as though God lowers His standards. His name needs to be cleared : how can He remain holy *and* accept the defiled? There is no question more vital.

No problem?
Some, of course, see no problem, for all they think necessary

is a change of heart in us. Let people be truly sorry and the basic problem is resolved. This is rather like the attitude of some parents when their child has done wrong. They are in a dilemma, feeling they should do something about it, but wanting to be kind. Perhaps they are reacting against their own up-bringing on the lines of 'being cruel to be kind' or 'this hurts me more than it hurts you'. They now feel that love and understanding are the great things, so they end by giving a gentle explanation and extracting an assurance: 'No, Daddy, I promise I won't do that again.' 'Good,' Daddy says, 'then that's fine.' Now the psychology employed by such parents is dubious to say the least; but even worse is the theology of those who think that God deals with sinful men and women in this way.

If parents persist with harmless chats and fail to deal with wrong, they are *un*kind to their children. Appropriate punishment may be a proof of love. It is a sign that parents care. Helen Lee[1] tells of a warden in a home for deprived and orphan boys. He brought up his own son along with the others and tried his hardest to love and treat them all equally. One day a boy reproached him: 'You don't love me as much as your boy, do you?' Feeling grieved, the warden asked, 'What makes you say that?' 'When *he* does something naughty, you give him a hiding,' came the reply. 'When I do, you just tell me off a bit.'

God cares

God cares about sin in people. In His holiness He cares so much, that all sin must have its due punishment. If He acquits sinners, His verdict must be consistent with His total opposition to sin. It must be based on justice and show Him to be just. A verdict on any other basis could not stand. Now the justice of a verdict is relevant even on a human level. A sharp-witted crime reporter may sense that something is not quite right with a particular acquittal, so he begins to sniff out the facts – the judge was bribed or someone purposely suppressed evidence. In that case the trial must be re-opened.

[1] Adapted from Helen Lee, *The Growing Years* (Falcon Books, 1963), p. 16.

The accused is now convicted on the basis of the full evidence. When the judge is in the wrong, the acquittal he pronounces is invalid, even if he did it from humanitarian motives.

Now God cannot justify anyone by bending the rules or neglecting the evidence – not if He is to stay true to His own nature. God's verdict must rest on justice, not on any lowering of His standards. This is vital for the name of God as well as for our security. The glory of the gospel is that He has made a way to justify us which He bases on a perfect obedience leading to a perfect sacrifice. But the obedience and the sacrifice are not ours; they are Christ's. A. M. Toplady summed it up: 'My Saviour's obedience and blood hide all my transgressions from view.'[2] The Bible works out for us these two aspects of the Lord's great work.

Pure obedience
God's Son became man in obedience. The purpose for which He came into this world comes out in the Letter to the Hebrews: 'when Christ came into the world, he said, . . . "Here I am . . . I have come to do your will, O God"' (Heb. 10 :5–7). It takes humility to obey, and Christ humbled Himself and took the form of a servant. Voluntarily He accepted as His duty the way of submission to His Father. He became obedient all the way through His earthly years up to and through a hideous, cruel death (Phil. 2 :6–8). He learnt this pure obedience. This does not mean, as it does when *we* learn to obey, that He had previously been rebellious. But He had not been along this way before. He had not known testing or suffering. He had not been made man before, and in this new situation he learnt obedience in experience through what He suffered (Heb. 5 :8, 9).

This is something marvellous for us. In Christ we do not see the best that rebel humanity could produce. Rather we face in Him the perfect revelation of God the Father. His life 'is all obedience, and therefore it is all revelation'.[3] All He

[2] From the hymn 'A debtor to mercy alone' by A. M. Toplady (1740–78).
[3] James Denney, *The Death of Christ* (Tyndale Press, 1951), p. 122.

says and does discloses His Father's mind; this is part of the reason why 'anyone who has seen me has seen the Father' (Jn. 14 :9).

All this is in sharp contrast to men. Great leaders of thought or action have all claimed some originality. They had a new insight or a fresh emphasis or a novel policy. But Christ did not so much claim to be original as to be obedient to His Father. His two great commands (to love God and to love one's neighbour, Mt. 22 :37–40) were not new – they are found in the Old Testament in Deuteronomy 6 :5 and Leviticus 19 :18. In His temptation He could surely have rebutted the devil in some original way. Instead He submitted to the Old Testament as the word of His Father; with that He overcame temptation (see Mt. 4 :1–11). He accepted the authority of the Old Testament and used it obediently to refute the Pharisees' misinterpretations. He did this, for example, on the subject of marriage when He asked them 'Haven't you read' what God said? (Mt. 19 :4). He did it also as regards duties to parents when He stated 'You have let go of the commands of God and are holding on to the traditions of men' (Mk. 7 :8). He accepted the Old Testament because this was one aspect of obedience. His Father's word was binding on Him.

This obedience comes out as Christ explains the origin of His teaching. He did not think it up on His own; rather He passed on what His Father said. 'I did not speak of my own accord, but the Father who sent me commanded me what to say and how to say it. . . . So whatever I say is just what the Father has told me to say' (Jn. 12 :49, 50).

Christ also explains His actions in terms of this obedience. 'The Son can do nothing by himself; he can do only what he sees his Father doing, because whatever the Father does the Son also does' (Jn. 5 :19). 'By myself I can do nothing; I judge only as I hear' (Jn. 5 :30). When He went to the Temple in Jerusalem at the age of twelve, He stayed behind as His parents set out for home. For this they later rebuked Him. His reply was not unkind; it just showed amazement that they did not know that 'I had to be in my Father's house' – on His Father's business (Lk. 2 :49). He had come to obey.

Everything He said and did, thought and desired was in direct obedience to the Father. Not grudging obedience, but obedience from the heart, unforced and free. In Him there was no sin at all. He lived the life we should have lived. He alone fully gave what God's law requires from all men : pure obedience.

Perfect sacrifice

Christ's death was the perfect sacrifice for sin – perfect because of the life that led up to it. He came to death, never once having fallen to temptation. At no time was He defiled or corrupted. Of all humanity He alone could offer Himself to God without fault. And being without sin, He came to death as the only one on whom death had no claim.

The death of such a person needs explanation – and many answers have been given. Some say He died because circumstances got out of His control – He had not reckoned on the people turning against Him. But the Bible denies this absolutely. He was delivered up, not captured as a helpless victim. And He was delivered up according to God's set purpose and foreknowledge (Acts 2 :23).

Many have said He died in order to exert a moral influence – to persuade us to spend our lives for others. It was to set an example of love which remained steadfast through opposition. Peter certainly saw that Christ suffered 'leaving you an example' (1 Pet. 2 :21). But these do not adequately explain why He should *die*. We could just as well argue that a long life of selfless service would have been an equal inspiration to us. After all, most Christians do not die a martyr's death when relatively young. It is often harder to follow Christ in middle or old age than in the idealism of youth. Yet He died a young man. A better explanation is needed.

Others say that He died to prove His love to the needy. But His death proves His love only if it is related to our need and guilt. James Denney illustrated this point : 'If I were sitting on the end of a pier on a summer day enjoying the sunshine and air, and some one came along and jumped into the water and got drowned "to prove his love for me", I should find it quite unintelligible. I might be much in need of love, but an act in no rational relation to any of my necessities could not prove it. But if I had fallen over the pier and were drowning, and some one sprang into the water, and at the cost of making ... my fate his own, saved me from death, then I should say, "Greater love hath no man than this." I should say it intelligibly, because there would be an intelligible relation between the sacrifice which love made and the necessity from which it redeemed.'[4]

In a similar way Christ's death is related to our sin. He died as the substitute for sinners, taking the guilt of others. He died, the righteous for the unrighteous. He became a curse for us (1 Pet. 3:18; Gal. 3:13). This is why the Bible makes 'Jesus Christ and him *crucified*' (1 Cor. 2:2) central. In fact the Bible is even more specific: its repeated stress is on the *blood* of Christ. Toplady's hymn, already mentioned, reflects this perfectly: 'My Saviour's obedience *and blood* hide all my transgressions from view.'

Christ reminds us of this every time we come to His table: 'This cup is the new covenant in my blood' (1 Cor. 11:25). Paul reminded the Ephesian elders that the Lord purchased the church with His own blood (Acts 20:28). He told the Romans that God put forward Christ 'as a sacrifice of atonement, through faith in his blood' (Rom. 3:25). We are justified by His blood (Rom. 5:9). John said that it is the blood of Jesus, God's Son, that 'purifies us from every sin' (1 Jn. 1:7). Hebrews says that the blood of Christ cleanses our consciences (Heb. 9:14), and sums it all up by asserting that 'without the shedding of blood there is no forgiveness' of sins (Heb. 9:22).

These writers emphasize Christ's blood because it points to a life violently *ended*. It is a strong way of speaking of death, and a specific way, too. It does not refer to death by accident or old age or ill-health, but to a penal, sacrificial death. Death as the punishment of sin, death to satisfy the broken law of God. This is why Paul links blood with propitiation

[4] James Denney, *op. cit.*, p. 103.

to explain Christ's death. It is a *propitiation* (that is, it turns away God's wrath) as well as an *expiation* (removing our sin). The difference is that you propitiate a person, you expiate a wrong. Christ's blood does both. It propitiates God and so secures His favour for believing sinners; and it expiates our wrong and so cancels our guilt.

No change in God

Propitiation does not mean that there is a change in God from a frown to a smile. After all, He planned our redemption through Christ's blood in eternity and He is always the same. It is simply that God cannot accept sinners if their sin is unpunished. If He did *that*, He would have changed. Christ's blood satisfies the just demands of God and establishes that God's attitude to sin is still one of total hatred. So the blood speaks of that death.

In other contexts, blood could refer to life. This is what many have argued about the term's use in Scripture. They say it is a picture of life – the blood pulsating through the veins of someone in full health and vigour. On this notion, Christ offered His manhood of flesh and *blood* to God for a life of service. He did that, of course. But this is not how the Bible uses the word 'blood'. It refers to death. Blood means life laid down in death, blood *shed*. Whatever the popular song says, it is not true that 'man shall live for evermore because of Christmas Day'. Only Christ's shed blood removes sin.

This word also sends us back to the Old Testament. The blood of bulls and goats was shed in sacrifices for the people's sins (Heb. 9:13), the blood of such sacrifices being substituted for that of offenders. There was no perfect or permanent forgiveness through such means, yet they instilled into successive generations in Israel this great principle: only the blood of a substitute can remove sins. These sacrifices all pointed to two facts: the *need* of a perfect sacrifice to make an end of sin; and the *manner* of it, by a substitute's blood.

Also a victory

Christ's death was substitutionary and it was also triumphant. Death claims everyone in the end as of right, for 'the soul that sins shall die' (Ezk. 18:4). We cannot avoid it, because none of us can atone for our sin. We can never make amends. Present obedience cannot cancel past rebellion. For us, death is the legal consequence of our sin, never a sacrifice for it. But while we have no choice in this matter, Christ *chose* to die. 'No one takes (my life) from me, but I lay it down of my own accord. I have authority to lay it down and authority to take it up again. This command I received from my Father' (Jn. 10:18). Christ could go to the devil and death and say : 'You have no power at all against me. I have come to death freely. I have come to taste it fully in the place of others. I will have to cry, "My God, my God, why have you forsaken me?" because I will be made sin for others. I will drain that cup to the last drop. But *you* are bound. And I am coming to take from your clutches a host of your captives. As their representative I accept the curse of death. Their punishment becomes mine. My sacrifice is perfect and complete. There is nothing you can do' (see Jn. 19:11; Heb. 2:9; Mt. 27:46; 12:29; Eph. 4:8; Gal. 3:13). This is why Christ said 'It is finished' (Jn. 19:30). That was a cry of victory, not defeat. The devil and death were finished, not Christ.

Christ thus gave His life as a ransom for many, to pay the price of their deliverance (Mk. 10:45). He bore in His own crucified body the sins that would have carried us to judgment (1 Pet. 2:24). He answered the charges levelled against us and so cancelled them (Col. 2:14).

When a man was to be crucified, a board was prepared. This gave the name or title of the condemned man, together with the charges against him. This placard was normally strung round the criminal's neck as he was led to his cross and then nailed to the wood above his head. Everyone could see who was being executed and why. And when the man died, all could see that the law had been satisfied and justice done in respect of those charges. When Christ died such a charge was nailed over His head : 'This is Jesus (His identity), the King of the Jews (the charge against Him)' (Mt. 27 :37). That was only the superficial reason for His execution. Metaphorically, all the charges of God's law against *sinners* were nailed to Christ's cross, so advertising to us that He died for our guilt.

His death thus declares that God's law has been satisfied and justice done in respect of His accusations against us. *This* is why it is a death of love. He acted as our proxy and stood in as our substitute. He did not die as an isolated individual, but as our Representative and Head. He gave His perfect life for a countless number from every century and every part of His world. His life was of such infinite worth that He, the one just man, has brought an infinite number of the unjust to God (1 Pet. 3 :18).

So Christ the righteous came to live and die in obedience for us. The Father did not spare His only Son anything (Rom. 8 :32). 'The Lord has laid on him the iniquity of us all' (Is. 53 :6). The Son willingly, for the joy that was set before Him, endured the cross and scorned its shame (Heb. 12 :2).

No bending the rules
No longer can anyone say that God bends His rules or lowers His standards. The cross satisfies His most pure and inflexible demands. This is how God can justify. The cross proves that He is just and righteous – as much opposed to sin as ever, true to His every word against sin and evil. But now His Son has for ever satisfied His law. So the cross also shows that He is the justifier of those who believe in His Son.

When God acquits anyone on *that* basis it is valid. It stands for eternity. Nothing can cancel it. Only a defect in Christ's obedience could revoke it; but there is no such flaw. Now 'God cannot but accept into His favour those who are invested with the righteousness of Christ'.[5] Christ was made sin for us; our sin was not His, but was reckoned to Him. We are accounted the righteousness of God in Him; His righteousness is not ours by nature, but is imputed to us (2 Cor. 5 :21).

[5] John Murray, *Redemption, Accomplished and Applied* (Eerdmans, 1955), p. 124.

James Denney said that 'but for Christ and His death, God would not be to us what He is'. But Christ has died and God is just when He justifies sinners. The gospel seems to violate His justice, but in fact it reveals it, and gloriously. Paul uses a potent word about this in Romans 3:25. The RSV weakly says that His death was 'to show God's righteousness'. Paul means that God gave a great *demonstration* of His righteousness; He proved it, presented it, put in on display. The cross broadcasts that His whole character is vindicated *and* that He saves men.

If sinners are condemned, then God is vindicated – but none is saved. If God's law is set aside, then we are accepted – but God is no longer God. Now, however, God has achieved both : He is proved to be both just and the justifier. This is no back-door way into heaven, avoiding the entrance requirements. He has given us direct access on the basis of His Son's death. 'A righteous God *and* a Saviour; there is none besides me' (Is. 45:21). 'The Lord is *our* righteousness' (Je. 23:6).

In Christ God has given us His own righteousness. This is His sovereign action – but what moved Him to do it *for us*?

4 Why all this for me?

Why did God go to all this trouble? Here is one answer.

At the very beginning there was 'nothing. A void.

'It must have been dull for God. I've thought so since a child. I was the sort of child who liked to know why and I once asked a learned uncle why God made the world.

'My uncle thought hard. My aunt too. I waited. They were both very clever.

'Then my uncle said, "Well, he had to do something. To occupy himself." And my aunt said, "You ask *why*? Tell me, why *not*?" . . .

'And the thought was planted . . . A God who'd been by himself for a long time. A quiet, thoughtful God, feeling sort of empty. A bit bored perhaps. Maybe even lonely. Sitting silent, still. And then suddenly thinking, "I know, I'll make a world. I need to do something to occupy myself. Why not?"

'Then he smiled. "That's it," he said, "I'll make someone to talk to . . .".'[1]

No compulsion

Some people are like that, always craving company, always needing someone to need them. But God is under no such compulsion. He is the only Person who is absolutely free, totally independent, wholly self-sufficient. He gives life, breath and everything else to all men, but has no needs Himself (Acts 17:25). Even if God did have needs, we could not supply them, for we have only what He has first given us. So God says, 'If I were hungry, I would not tell you; for

[1] David Kossoff, *Bible Stories* (Fontana, 1971), pp. 11–13.

39

the world and all that is in it is mine' (Ps. 50 : 12). He seeks those who will worship in spirit and truth, but He does not depend on them (Jn. 4 : 23).

He did not need to create man and He did not need to redeem man. It is the grossest distortion to propose a God who is bored, lonely and unfulfilled without us. You know how you felt as a child when you passed the pet shop. You saw the last puppy of the litter left in the window, all sad and droopy. You couldn't help feeling sorry for him – and we cannot help feeling sorry for such a poor little 'deity'. No, God did not go to this trouble because He needed company, as pop-stars need fans. He went to this length because of His grace.

The grace of God

The Bible tells us much about what grace is : God's favour to the condemned. It is favour which is unasked, unwanted and undeserved – but desperately needed. It is more than God being well-disposed to us – it is His favour in action, actually saving sinners from condemnation and hell. The Bible is full of it, describing the need it meets, the judgment it averts, the benefits it brings and the heaven it opens. But there is no explanation of grace. None. From what the Bible says it seems to me that we shall not know the full explanation of grace, even in heaven. We shall spend eternity in unceasing wonder at the inexpressible grace of God in Christ. Certainly we shall never come to the point of saying, 'That's it. I know it now. I've got it all figured out.' Rather we will say, 'O the depth of the riches, the wisdom and the knowledge of God! How unsearchable his judgments, and his paths beyond tracing out!' (Rom. 11 : 33). Grace will remain amazing for ever. The redeemed will always ask, 'But why all this to me?'

Yet the mystery of *why* does not alter the reality of grace. 'By grace you *have been* saved' (Eph. 2 : 5). Sins and evil desires filled our life, though often we hid them under the disguise of respectability; we waved the flags of progress, change and knowledge, but in fact were following the devil's way (Eph. 2 : 1–3). We were slaves to sin; indeed it had killed us. But that was not all. Paul trumpets out his earth-shaking 'But'. 'But God,' he says. Not, as we should expect, 'but God came in judgment'. Rather this : 'But because of his great love for us, God, who is rich in mercy, made us alive with Christ even when we were dead in transgressions – it is by grace you have been saved' (Eph. 2 :4, 5).

God acted purely out of grace to justify the ungodly. On the positive side He did so to put on display what His kindness could do for dead rebels (Eph. 2 :7). On the negative side He did so to rule out all possibility that anyone should brag about themselves before Him (Eph. 2 :9; 1 Cor. 1 :29–31). God acted expressly to exclude our boasting. In heaven no-one will be able to say, 'I'm here because of my character or deeds ... my giving to charity ... my activity for God.' Equally no-one will be able to say, 'I couldn't be here apart from Christ's death; He made it possible, but it was my faith that clinched it.' In heaven everyone will say, with utter joy and no quibble, 'by the grace of God I am what I am' (1 Cor. 15 :10). William Temple once wrote that the only thing 'I can contribute to my salvation is the sin from which I need to be saved'. His meaning is clear; obviously God does not contribute our sins. But the Bible drops the notion of contributing altogether. 'From him and through him and to him are all things. To him be the glory for ever !' (Rom. 11 :36). Justification is by grace from beginning to end. Every single thing that gets a person to heaven comes from God.

Horrid charity ?
Until the Holy Spirit opens our eyes, 'grace' is offensive to us. To live on charity is humiliating. On the human level this comes out in E. Nesbit's *The Railway Children*. The station porter, Perks, was very poor – so poor that he had never had presents on his birthday. The three children went round the villagers, requesting presents to give to Perks. But when they produced them, he was mortally offended. The children brought them with the best of intentions, but he would have none of them. 'So you've been round telling the neighbours we can't make both ends meet ? Well, now you've

disgraced us as deep as you can in the neighbourhood ...
Do you think I've kept respectable and outer debt on what
I gets ... to be given away for a laughing-stock to all the
neighbours?' The only way the children could find to persuade him at last to accept the gifts was to say : nobody who
gave a present 'said anything about charity or anything
horrid like that'.

Unilateral declaration

God's charity is not horrid but glorious. It is also unique. It
is not found in any of the world's cults or religions, nor in
much of what passes for Christianity. From the Pharisees'
stress on deeds to the mystics' focus on meditation, all
religions emphasize human achievement. They are all bi-
lateral agreements : God does part, we do part. God gives the
revelation; man supplies the faith, the prayer and the devotion. God gives the cross; we bring our decision. But the God
of Christianity is a God of unilateral action. In 1965
Rhodesia made her Unilateral Declaration of Independence.
Whatever the rights and wrongs of her controversial action,
it did not come about by consultation, conference or bargaining; Rhodesia acted on her own. And God acted on His
own, making a unilateral declaration of grace.

Prophets and apostles assert this. The Reformers do also.
To them 'the crucial question was not simply, whether God
justifies believers without works of law. It was the broader
question, whether sinners are wholly helpless in their sin,
and whether God is to be thought of as saving them by free,
unconditional, invincible grace.'[2]

Grace to accept grace

It takes grace to accept grace. One individual put it like
this : 'In the last resort this wounds our self-love, this receiving of what we do not deserve. And this is why we have
difficulty accepting it. We would prefer to have merited it;

[2] From the 'Historical and Theological Introduction', by J. I.
Packer and O. R. Johnston, to Martin Luther, *The Bondage of the
Will* (James Clarke, 1957), pp. 58f.

we contend with God for the merit.'[3] Yet His grace is our only hope – and our certain hope. In justifying us He makes His eternal purpose real to us in time. Because of grace justification has this eternal dimension. It is God's verdict of the last day brought forward to now. We do not keep God in suspense until we do (or do not) respond. He does not keep us in suspense until the final day. His grace is decisive.

In His grace God planned justification in eternity, but brought it to us only in time. It is within our living experience that His justifying word is heard. The question is, how do we come to hear and know this verdict? How is justification received? How does grace make it part of our experience?

[3] Paul Tournier, *Guilt and Grace* (Hodder and Stoughton, 1962), p. 195.

5 How come?

A man had fallen over the pier and could not swim. He desperately needed someone to rescue him – and the action of his rescuer is a picture of grace. It was his love and power that saved the drowning man. But there is also the question of how the sinking man would experience his rescue.

However much he hoped to see his family again, he could not be saved by *hoping*. However much he loved his rescuer, he could not be brought to safety by *loving* (though afterwards he would have lasting love and gratitude). However many instructions he received, he would not be saved by *his own effort*, for he was helpless in the water. He was saved only as he stopped flailing his arms in futile self-help and *trusted* his rescuer. Then he would feel gratitude and love and hope and joy. But in his rescue the only appropriate attitude was trust.

The Bible says justification is simply through faith. 'By grace' tells us why it comes to us; 'through faith' tells us how we receive it. Grace and faith explain and complement each other. But what is faith? The word has so many uses and abuses.

Inborn attitude?

To some it is a natural, inborn attitude. Dr Lloyd-Jones[1] describes this as the view which says, ' "We all have faith. When you sit down on a chair you are exercising faith . . . When you go for a ride on a train or bus you are exercising faith." The argument is that we all have faith, and that all we need

[1] D. M. Lloyd-Jones, *Romans: An Exposition of Chapters 3:20 – 4:25; Atonement and Justification* (Banner of Truth, 1970), p.232.

to do is to exercise that faith that is innate in human nature, in the matter of believing in God.' As he says, however, that is not faith in God but just a calculation of the probabilities (it's a million to one against an accident) or a blind optimism (it'll never happen to me).

Leap in the dark?

To others, faith means a leap in the dark. 'Suppose we were climbing in the Alps and were very high on the bare rock and suddenly the fog shuts down. The guide . . . says that before morning we will all freeze to death here on the shoulder of the mountain . . . None of us has any idea where we are. After an hour or so, someone says to the guide : 'Suppose I dropped and hit a ledge ten feet down in the fog. What would happen then?" The guide would say that you might make it till the morning and thus live. So, with absolutely no knowledge or any reason to support his action, one of the group hangs and drops into the fog. This would be one kind of faith, a leap of faith.'[2] Such people say that we cannot know God or prove Him. Reason cannot help. We must just make some commitment – to a new sect, or a new lifestyle, or drugs; then we will find reality and identity. But that is not faith, just foolhardiness.

Being religious?

Faith to some means being religious and going to church. This can even be thought of as a good insurance policy, just in case we have to meet God in an after-life.

In some contexts 'believing in' something means little more than approving it – 'I believe in the royal family . . . or in democracy.' That just means that they think royalty or Parliament a good thing. Other folk say, 'I believe in God. I've got faith. After all, I'm not an atheist.' That, however, only means 'I believe there is a God'. That is intellectual assent to a proposition, not faith. Faith certainly involves reason, is based on true propositions, and is no irrational leap. It comes by hearing the word of God (Rom.

[2] F. A. Schaeffer, *He is There and He is Not Silent* (Hodder and Stoughton, 1972), p. 95.

10 : 17) and thoughtfully receiving it. It does not excuse any-one from thought, but it is never mere assent.

Trust

Faith is trust in a Person, *the* Person, God Himself. In New Testament terms it is explicitly faith in the Son of God, the Lord Jesus Christ.

It was in this sense that Abraham had faith. He acknow-ledged the existence of God, but more than that, he be-lieved the Lord (Gn. 15 : 6). He trusted Him and cast him-self totally on God's wisdom and promise, grace and power. The tax-collector of whom Jesus spoke had similar faith as he stood in the Temple beating his breast in shame. 'God, have mercy on me, a sinner' were his words of trust in God (Lk. 18 : 13). Christ looked for this when He said we were to 'become like little children' (Mt. 18 : 3) and exercise child-like trust.

Children have to trust others because they cannot cope for themselves; but there is no need or place for trust when we can manage on our own. I can easily change the wheel when my car has a flat tyre; but when the oil seal on the differential leaks, I am in trouble. That repair is beyond me and I trust the mechanics.

Our resources exhausted

Trust begins only when we come to an end of ourselves. Abraham came to an end of himself, for he could not con-jure up the son God had promised him when Sarah was too old. The tax-collector was at an end of himself, for he could not wipe out his guilt. The prodigal exhausted his own resources and came to his senses only when he 'began to be in need'. Then he said, 'How many of my father's hired men have food to spare, and here I am starving to death!' (Lk. 15 : 14, 17). At one time Paul was under the illusion that he had kept every command of God perfectly. But then he saw that this supposed credit with God was as worthless as rubbish. He came to an end of trying to work up his own righteousness (Phil. 3 : 6, 7).

That is where faith begins, at the point where we despair

46

of saving ourselves. This has two consequences. First, *faith is not righteousness.* It is not as though God says, 'I will accept either the righteousness My law demands or faith in Christ. As you cannot supply the righteousness, I will take faith as its equivalent.' Christ alone is our righteousness. Faith is simply trust in the One who is righteous. God-righteousness (as distinct from self-righteousness) comes to us through faith.

Secondly, *faith is not a work.* That is, it is not something we produce to earn merit for ourselves with God. Now no-one who accepts the Bible would say it is, and yet sometimes Christians present the gospel like this : 'In theory there are two ways of being accepted with God. You can try the way of works; you can try by what you do to achieve a credit balance with God. But as you can never do perfect works all the time, that way is impossible. So you must take the other way, the way of faith. You offer your faith to God and God will respond to your faith by taking you in.'

If we could ask a Pharisee, 'Why do you think you are accepted with God?' he would answer, 'Because I have kept what the law requires.' He would answer with reference to himself – 'Because I . . .'. Ask the same question in Christian circles and some answers will begin in the same way : 'Because *I* surrendered . . . Because *I* have decided to follow Jesus . . . Because *I* went to the front at the close of the meeting . . . Because *I* gave my life to Christ.'

Now the Bible is very clear that sinners must *believe* in Christ and that such faith must be personal and *decisive.* There is a universe of difference between belief and unbelief. Paul spends a long time urging on the Roman Christians the importance of faith. Nothing is more important for an individual than that he should put faith in Christ. But Paul also spends a long time showing what he means by saving faith. He rejects the idea of trying to twist God's arm by bringing forward our works – or our faith. Justification is not a business transaction in which God contracts to supply forgiveness if we agree to pay in our faith. There is only one Saviour : it is not a co-operative effort. It is Christ who saves : neither my works nor my decision,

47

neither my efforts nor my response, neither my zeal nor my faith. As soon as I say anything like 'I am a Christian because *I* . . .', I am saying something other than 'I am a Christian because *Christ* . . .'.

No Christian wants to say that; and we should be clearer in our thinking, more grateful for our salvation and more zealous in our service if we dropped that whole attitude. Faith is not a work. This is not an academic matter, for this line of thought gets many Christians into difficulties. It affects the person who fears that he is not a Christian because his faith is shaky : 'If only my faith were stronger, then I'm sure I'd be sure.' Clearly there is a link between faith and assurance. Clearly weak faith is both wrong and unfortunate. But the trouble for that person is that his attention is all on the state of his faith. He is back to thinking that it depends on him, and that is the opposite of faith. Always to be thinking about faith only shows that something is wrong. To concentrate on faith is doubt, for true faith is taken up with God. 'Hudson Taylor used to say that you should translate one of Christ's sayings, not as "Have faith in God", but "Hold on to the faithfulness of God". The reference is to God.'[3]

Crediting God with power

This is what Abraham's faith did. He certainly thought about his own state at times; he considered his age and Sarah's barrenness. Yet his faith grew strong only as he thought about God. He gave glory to God (Rom. 4:20); that is, he credited God with the power and will and grace to do what He had promised. His mind was on God, and that was faith.

While Peter looked at Christ, he was able to walk on the water. When he looked round (and suddenly saw what an incredible thing he was doing) he began to sink (Mt. 14:29, 30). But with his eyes on Christ, he walked; that was faith. So we must jettison the idea of bringing or offering faith to God in place of works. The whole point of faith is not faith itself but the God who is trusted.

[3] D. M. Lloyd-Jones, *op. cit.*, p. 234.

48

Such faith is personal. Dean Inge was right when he said, 'One cannot be religious by proxy.'[4] Faith cannot be second-hand, but must be *my* faith, *your* faith. Personal trust means recognizing that the only alternative to works is not even faith, but God Himself. 'Not the labours of my hands . . . Thou must save, and Thou alone.'[5]

Faith and works
This view of faith is confirmed when we look at its opposite and see the meaning of 'works'. In contrast to faith, 'works' means anything that comes from us while we are apart from God. Anything we think we can contribute to our salvation – good intentions, good deeds, our profession of faith, our piety, even our baptism. Specifically 'works of law' means obedience to God's moral law, especially the Ten Commandments. No-one will be accepted because of such works. In theory they might be, if they perfectly kept the law in outward conduct and inward motives. But only Christ could keep the law like that. Our failure drives us to say, ' I know that nothing good lives in me' (Rom. 7 : 18). And if there is anything good about us, we must listen to Paul asking : 'What do you have that you did not receive?' (1 Cor. 4 : 7).

The devil knows that works cannot save and so he has always concentrated people's attention on them. A stress on outward actions or rites is the commonest error in religion. The Jews relied on their circumcision and law-keeping; monks on their monastic life; some still today on their church-going – but it is the same fault, a dependence on works.

'Through faith' therefore means 'by God'. I come to see that I cannot, but He can. I have not, but He has. John Bunyan put it like this : 'If the justification of their persons is by, in, and through Christ; then it is not by, in, and through their own doings.'[6]

[4] Cited in Louis Bouyer, *The Spirit and Forms of Protestantism* (Harvill Press, 1956), p. 98.
[5] From the hymn 'Rock of ages' by A. M. Toplady.
[6] John Bunyan, *Justification by an Imputed Righteousness; or, No way to heaven but by Jesus Christ* (Collected Works, various editions).

Faith is often described as the instrument of our justification, or as the means by which we appropriate it, or as the open hand stretched out to receive it. These phrases are helpful, so long as we never think that our faith causes our salvation. God causes it; He saves. Faith is not a condition to fulfil, so that when we believe we can say, 'Now I qualify.' 'By faith' is rather God's way of conditioning us. It shows us the spirit which alone is fitting before God. It leads us to the only right attitude to our guilt and His grace. Saving faith is not creative, but receptive. It does not make our salvation, it takes it gratefully.

Contrast

The contrast between faith and works is therefore like this. Works see God as indebted to us because we deserve His favour; faith sees us as indebted to God because of His undeserved grace. Works express optimism about myself : if I try hard enough, I'll make it; faith expresses despair of myself : my efforts can never save me. Works write off God's grace as unnecessary; faith writes off my righteousness as filthy rags. Works stress *me*; faith stresses *Christ*. So Luther, commenting on Galatians 5 :14, wrote that it is 'impossible that Christ and the law should dwell together in one heart; for either the law or Christ must give place'.

In all these ways 'through faith' underlines 'by grace'. The fact that we must first perceive in order to believe further emphasizes this. Not, of course, in the literal sense of seeing, on which doubting Thomas insisted. We do not need to see Christ's risen body, but we must perceive the truth. Without that, we shall never believe, because we shall never see our need to believe. Jesus was emphatic that it is only when a man is born again that he can *see* the Kingship of God. That perception is what Jesus mentions first. Then He adds that without this new birth no-one can *enter* (Jn. 3 :3, 5). New birth is necessary to give insight and entry.

An illustration of this comes in the incident in which Christ gave sight to the man born blind. After being healed the man said : 'I do know one thing : I was blind but now I see !' This was even more than restored eyesight, for when he saw he said, 'Lord, I believe' and worshipped Him (Jn. 9:25, 38). Blind sinners see spiritually only when God gives them vision. 'For God who said, "Let light shine out of darkness," made his light shine in our hearts to give us the light of the knowledge of the glory of God in the face of Christ' (2 Cor. 4:6).

It is the Holy Spirit who brings this light to us. He came to convince people of sin (Jn. 16:8). He puts us in the dock and brings the force of God's accusations to our conscience. He cross-examines us so that we feel worthy only of summary condemnation. Like a prosecuting counsel, He presses home the guilt of not believing in Christ until we feel despair. We cannot see or feel things that way ourselves, for that whole view is entirely foreign to us before the Spirit begins to work in us. So this is His work, as it was when He convicted the hearts of Peter's hearers at Pentecost, making them cry out, 'What shall we do?' (Acts 2:37).

It is the Spirit of God who convinces us that Christ has dealt with sin and provided His righteousness for us. He proves this to us by showing us that the Father received His Son back into glory and, in doing so, set His approval on Christ's work. He further convinces us that Christ has overcome and judged the devil, so that no power can now tear us from Christ. Thus the Holy Spirit gives us life and sight and leads us to Christ. (And, incidentally, it is because the Spirit so convinces us of the awfulness of sin that as believers we can never sin again so lightly or glibly.)

From God

We know the devils 'believe'; they know that there is a God and they shudder at the thought (Jas. 2:19). Many people similarly assent to certain affirmations, but this does not mean they have saving trust. Now it is certainly our duty to believe, and 'without faith it is impossible to please God' (Heb. 11:6). Yet our pride will not let us trust, for 'those controlled by their sinful nature cannot please God' (Rom. 8:8). This is why Jesus said, 'No one can come to me unless the Father who sent me draws him' (Jn. 6:44). And again, 'No one knows the Father except the Son and those to whom the Son chooses to reveal him'. But because Jesus has that power, He at once gives the gracious invitation, 'Come to me, all you who are weary' (see Mt. 11 :27, 28).

Saving faith comes from God. It is only when God works in us by His Spirit that we can trust. Salvation is thus by grace 'through faith – and this not from yourselves, it is the gift of God' (Eph. 2 :8).

Faith alone
All this shows why Martin Luther was right to translate 'justification by faith' as 'justification by faith alone'. Now the 'alone' is technically an addition to the text of Scripture and the opponents of his teaching pounced on this. 'If anyone says that a sinful man is justified by faith alone, meaning that no other co-operation is required to obtain the grace of justification . . . let him be anathema.'[7] 'If anyone says that justifying faith is nothing else than confidence that divine Mercy remits sins for Christ's sake . . . let him be anathema.'[8] But 'when taken to task for this liberty, Luther replied that . . . the extra word was necessary in German to bring out the force of the original'.[9]

The meaning 'alone' is there right enough. Indeed, much Roman Catholic teaching has to admit the meaning of Scripture on this, although it then goes on to bring in baptism or works alongside faith.[1] But when faith is subor-

---

[7] Council of Trent, *Canons on Justification*, 9.   [8] *Ibid.*, 12.
[9] Quoted in R. H. Bainton, *Here I Stand*, p. 261.
[1] Roman Catholic writers put the matter of saving faith in these terms. 'Faith is the "sole instrument",' said Newman (*op. cit.*, p. 261). 'The sinner is justified through faith alone,' wrote Küng (*op. cit.*, p. 243). But to such writers faith generally means assent; and works and observance of the sacraments are then added as also necessary for salvation. 'Faith is the "sole instrument" as preceded and made an instrument by the secret virtue of Baptism. St. Paul too, when he speaks of justification through faith, speaks of faith as subordinate to Baptism' (Newman, p. 260). 'What is all important is that faith and Baptism belong together' (Küng, p. 245). 'An assent to the doctrine that faith alone justifies does not at all preclude the doctrine of works justifying also', though obviously 'not in the same sense'! (Newman, p. 314). 'The sinner is justified through faith alone, but not through a faith which stands opposed to works' (Küng, p. 243).

dinated to baptism or supplemented by works, it is no more faith. True saving faith cannot be added to. The idea of faith *alone* is present in the contrasts and denials in Scripture. 'It is by grace you have been saved, through faith – and this' (here is the denial) 'not from yourselves . . . not by works, so that no one can boast' (Eph. 2 :8, 9). Boasting is excluded on the principle of faith. 'For we maintain that a man is justified by faith apart from' (the contrast) 'observing the law' (Rom. 3 :28).

'Alone' is part of the meaning of faith. If it is not faith only, it is not faith at all. Either I can bring something for my acceptance, or I cannot. If I can, then I can boast – and there is no trust involved. If I cannot, I must trust for everything; I must write off every other conceivable way to God and depend totally on Christ.

> 'Upon a life I did not live,
> Upon a death I did not die,
> Another's life, Another's death,
> I rest my whole eternity.'

Christ alone

The deepest reason for 'faith alone' is that salvation is 'by Christ alone'. Faith only means it is all Christ. Christ, not the church; Christ, not me; Christ alone. This is certainly the Bible's teaching. The trouble is that it seems to cut out my responsibility altogether. I *cannot* do anything to gain justification, for Christ does it all. I *need* not do anything, for faith rules out works. So the question arises : what are the consequences of this emphasis on grace and faith? What does 'faith only' lead to – a life of spiritual idleness?

We need to look at the responsibilities it brings, but before doing that we must look first at the benefits it yields.

6 What follows?

The direct result of being justified by faith is that we have peace with God (Rom. 5 : 1). This is the first consequence of justification; and it is so wonderful that we need to be very precise in the way we understand it. If our thinking is woolly, we shall neither enjoy our justification as we should nor give God proper thanks for it.

We hear much about peace. 'I'd give anything for peace of mind,' says a distracted society, swallowing another tranquillizer. 'I'll drown my worries,' says a frenzied world, as it gulps down another gin and tonic. 'Peace is my next fix,' says the addict. 'Real peace is Jesus,' says the sticker. The testimony says, 'I was dissatisfied and all churned up until I found peace in Jesus.' What is peace? To most people it means peace of mind : a psychological state in which they no longer fret, or a temperament which is always placid and unruffled, or the ability to look on the bright side.

Peace with God

This is not what Paul means by peace with God. He was not saying that 'Now I'm justified, I have a peaceful kind of feeling about life'. He was not talking about a state of mind, but a restored relationship – peace *with* God, not just peace. There is a difference. Many would give anything for peace, but not so many want peace with God. This is simply because, to be at peace with someone, you must meet and face them. This is why a football referee may make two players shake hands. One fouled, the other retaliated, and they must make it up and say 'Sorry'. Now the referee cannot eradicate the enmity of the players, but in principle he is right to make them face each other in apology. If they slipped away to opposite ends of the field, their vendetta would certainly flare up again. Peace with God means facing God – and the consequence of justification is that we *can* face Him and be at peace with Him.

Paul uses two phrases about peace : peace *with* God and the peace *of* God (Phil. 4 :7). The Christian knows also the peace *of* God. It passes all understanding. It surrounds and defends his heart like a garrison round a castle (Phil. 4 :7) and it teaches the Christian to be content whatever the circumstances (Phil. 4 :11). The mind thus stayed on God is kept in perfect peace, literally 'peace-peace', peace twice over (Is. 26 :3). That is the peace of God, enjoyed in daily experience and dealing with anxiety (1 Pet. 5 :7).

Peace *with* God is related to this, but there are practical reasons why we should keep to Paul's distinction. For example, Christians sometimes come into spiritual depression. Maybe they look back on a rather unconvincing conversion. They lack a sense of peace and fret more about the future than they used to. They feel uneasy about their faith and may come to doubt their whole relationship with God. All this may be due to their thinking, 'Because I don't feel peace I cannot be saved.' Though they may not know it, what that really means is : 'Because I don't feel the peace *of* God I cannot be at peace *with* God and cannot be a Christian.'

It is vital to be clear on this. We shall not always feel the same and our conscious enjoyment of the peace of God may vary. But peace with God is a constant for all who are justified. Paul tells us what peace with God is. To him it is a stupendous miracle for us to be at peace with the God we have wronged !

Peace with God is based on the fact that 'there is now no condemnation for those who are in Christ Jesus' (Rom. 8 :1). We have already looked at this aspect of justification. 'No condemnation' means this : no rejection at the day of judgment, no having to answer for our own sins, no hell, no outer darkness. It means God will not take issue with us then, for Christ has made peace by the blood of His cross. It means that no-one can bring any charge against those whom God has chosen: 'Who is he that condemns?' asks Paul, confident that nothing can separate us from the love of God in Christ (Rom. 8:33–35). It means that we need not be in terror before the devil nor tremble at the prospect of death.

Access

Along with the strong assurance of these negatives comes the positive meaning of peace with God. It means access: 'We have gained access by faith into this grace in which we now stand' (Rom. 5:2). Access is important in all areas of life. Access to the right people can open doors. This is why we do not want to be fobbed off by the office-girl when we have an important matter to discuss with the person in charge.

The Jews were once in danger of extermination in Babylon. Their fate hinged on whether they could get King Ahasuerus to change his mind. So the Queen Esther, a Jewess, had to gain access to him. But even for the queen to enter his presence without being called meant death. We can imagine the relief when he held out the golden sceptre (Est. 4:11; 8:4) and let her have audience. Access averted disaster.

Access was crucial to the paralysed man and his friends. They had to get to Jesus, but the crowds stood between them. So they took up the roof and let the man down. Access meant forgiveness and restoration (Mk. 2:1–12).

To have access means to be brought into someone's presence, especially to be brought before a king. There are many clubs to which only paid-up members have access. I may pass by their doors and envy their facilities, but I may not enter unless a member signs me in. Then, by his kindness, I can enjoy all they provide. When that member signs me in, he says, 'Put it down to my account.' And when I am inside, he introduces me to the other members: 'James, may I introduce my guest . . .?' Then the others talk among themselves: 'I say, did you see who old Perkins brought in tonight?' I am there always by reference to the one who brought me in.

Now justification means that Christ has signed us into His Father's presence. He made the staggering assertion that our names are written in God's family register in heaven (Lk. 10:20). He had the charges against us put down to Him; and He settled that account on the cross. Now He introduces us to the Father. We are His guests, not there in our own right but only by reference to Him. We are even called by His name : Christians, Christ's people. What an immense privilege this is !

So the access we have is not fleeting access on the odd occasion. In this grace we *stand*; it is our permanent position, for we live in the presence of God. His company is our environment. But this does not end all problems. Christ Himself had constant access to His Father, but had to face opposition and scorn, injustice and betrayal. Our Father may not always explain or help in the way we want. Yet Christ had access; and so, by grace, do we.

The word translated 'access' has a further dimension : it can refer also to a landing-stage. It implies that without God we are all at sea, tossed around by storms of doubt and guilt. Christ is the one who brings us to the shore; we come to the landing-stage and are at home with God, on solid ground. He has brought us to God.

Adoption

This is why God calls Himself 'our Father'. The thought of the Fatherhood of God is central to salvation, though not in the mistaken sense that He is everyone's Father whether they acknowledge Him or not. Only believers, but all believers, may call Him Father, because they are adopted. On the human level adoption is a legal matter. A couple may love a child intensely and have everything necessary to provide for it. Yet still the adoption must go through the court. If the court does not make the child legally theirs, it may later remove him, to the anguish of all concerned. It is similar with God. As Judge, He goes on record as declaring us adopted and enters our names in His family register (Lk. 10:20). He constitutes us legally His sons and daughters. We know then that 'the Father himself loves' us (Jn. 16:26) and so 'our fellowship is with the Father and with his Son,

Jesus Christ' (1 Jn. 1 :3). Justification sets up the basis for this marvellous Father-child relationship.

The Bible links the thoughts of access and adoption. Mari Jones saw this truth of adoption illustrated as she observed life on her Welsh sheep-farm. After a severe winter a weakened ewe sometimes gives birth and then leaves the lamb. She is not strong enough both to support herself and to suckle her lamb, and so the lamb becomes an orphan. Sometimes it also happens that a stronger ewe loses her lamb. In that case the shepherd flays the dead lamb very carefully, cuts five holes in the skin and then drapes it over the orphan. Then he puts it in a pen with the bereaved mother. She will begin to sniff the lamb thoroughly. At last the shepherd will see what he longs for : the skin has done its work. The mother adopts the lamb as her own.[1] She does so because she has been deceived. She smelt her own lamb and responded to that. But there is no deceit when God adopts us; His Son, the Lamb of God, died and covers us with His righteousness. We are adopted.

One of the loveliest descriptions of what follows from justification comes not from Paul but from Christ Himself in the synagogue at Nazareth. His reading from the scroll of Isaiah described His own ministry as a preacher of justification : 'The Spirit of the Lord is on me; therefore he has anointed me to preach good news to the poor. He has sent me to proclaim freedom for the prisoners and recovery of sight for the blind, to release the oppressed, to proclaim the year of the Lord's favour' (Lk. 4 :18, 19). Freedom from prison; the sight of Christ's glory; release from oppression; favour in place of rejection – these all spring from the access we have through peace with God.

New environment

With this access and adoption we have a new spiritual environment. We used to live in pride and self-will. Now that we have been justified, we belong where Christ is. Our life is hidden with Him in God and our citizenship is in heaven.

[1] Mari Jones, *In the Shadow of Aran* (Evangelical Movement of Wales, 1972), pp. 28f.

In this new environment we have a new perspective. We begin to see things as God does. New surroundings begin to have their effect on us. We cannot help being influenced by the values of heaven: its purity and light, its glory and power. All because of access.

Luther said that justification 'is the master and chief lord, ruler and judge of every kind of doctrine and one which preserves and directs every doctrine of the church'. It is also the truth which preserves and directs every experience of the Christian. It is the key to every facet of true spiritual experience. It is the key simply because it gives acccess to God. Access means prayer, brings assurance, creates joy, prompts thanksgiving, and opens to us the power and victory of God. Every blessing the Christian can know flows from the presence of God, into which justification brings us.

Access before accessories

In this chapter we are asking, 'What follows?' The stress is important: first comes justification, then its consequences. If we overlook this, we are heading for trouble. If we chase the blessings, they evaporate. If we seek power first, we shall in the end be disappointed. If we just want our wants, we shall feel let down. God does not give His smaller blessings first; He gives Himself.

That is how the Christian life begins and how it continues. His glory comes before our desires, the Giver before His gifts, the access before the accessories. Justification gets our priorities right at the outset and so allows all God's benefits to come into play in the Christian's life.

This is very practical and helps us, for example, when we get into doubt about our relationship with God. If we do not feel the peace of God, it is of prime importance that we should go back to the matter of our access. We should put to ourselves the basic questions: has Christ made peace by the blood of His cross? On whom, then, am I depending for my access to God? Am I trusting Christ alone? Is there anyone else I can trust? Do I face even death depending on Christ? We may still feel uneasy, but if we know the answers to these questions in our hearts, then we know that the foundation is secure.

This is what the Christian should do when he feels he is too unworthy to belong to God – he should look again at the worthiness of Christ and see how Christ brought him to God. This is what troubled Christians should do, instead of trying desperately to con themselves into peace of mind. This is what Christians who have been relying on their response or the mere date or manner of their conversion should do. This is what Christians should do if they are tempted to rely on 'signs' for their ease of mind. When we forget the access Christ secured and focus on other things, we must not be surprised if we go adrift.

Justification first, then its marvellous consequences of access and adoption. These are God's encouragements to everyone who trusts His Son. These favours, however, do not make us perfect; in fact, the more we use our access to God, the more we realize how deep-seated is our selfishness. The more we spend time in His company, the more shame-fully obvious is the contrast between His character and ours.

Now God has decreed that all the justified shall be con-formed in character to the likeness of His Son (Rom. 8:29, 30). Indeed, when Christ appears we shall be like Him (1 Jn. 3:2). God is concerned not just to 'get us saved' but also to get us changed. What then is the link between God's declar-ing us pardoned and making us righteous? And what does this tell us about our responsibilities to God?

7 Growing and doing

God has some very straight commands for those He has justified. For example, He says, 'Make every effort . . . to be holy; without holiness no one will see the Lord' (Heb. 12:14). On its own that sounds rather forbidding and dull, but it does not stand on its own. First comes access to God; that moves us to give thanks for all God has done; and thankfulness leads us to take up our responsibilities. God's commands to the believer always come in the context of grace and gratitude.

Access affects behaviour
This is how it works in that club mentioned in the last chapter. The fact that Perkins signs me in affects my behaviour. I am there as his guest and his good name in the club is at stake in me. If I am rude or churlish, he gets the blame; after all, the others will say, he brought me in. But in fact I so appreciate what he has done for me that I want my behaviour to please him. And it is similar in our relationship to God. Because Christ brought us in, we want to live in a way that is worthy of that calling (Eph. 4:1). It is a pleasure so to live that we make the truth about God our Saviour attractive (Tit. 2:10). Access to God is a stimulus to behave like Christ and to show love as He did.

To put it another way, justification leads into sanctification. God has set up an intimate bond between His declaring us righteous and making us righteous. The Bible gives us at least five links between the two facts of justification and sanctification.

Five links

First, there is the link we have mentioned : the same God purposes both. He 'has saved us' (justification) 'and called us to a holy life' (a calling to sanctification) (2 Tim. 1 :9).

Secondly, the one God achieves both. They are two facets of His one comprehensive work in which He saves from the guilt, slavery and presence of sin. In other words, it is God who justifies, sanctifies and glorifies. In justification He alters our status and then in sanctification He begins to change our character. Salvation is one work, not a random collection of bits and pieces. Yet God has revealed its successive stages so that we may understand our relation to His law (justification) and His life (sanctification). We may not divide these two aspects, which is why Paul sometimes puts these terms together : 'You were washed . . . sanctified . . . justified' (1 Cor. 6 :11). Equally, we must not confuse them.

A third link is that of faith. Since faith means trust in a Person, it does not end once an individual has been accepted. It is a living principle, a way of life. It is inconceivable to trust Christ for pardon and then refuse to trust Him for guidance or power. To trust Christ at all is to trust Him for all. Genuine trust goes on until glory, when faith gives way to sight. Our need to depend on Him will never lessen. Faith operates in both justification and sanctification. This does not mean that we receive entire sanctification 'by faith' in an instant, as we received our complete justification. Sanctification is a life of growing trust in God.

Fourthly, this means that justification is the beginning and sanctification the continuing. Justification is complete once for all; sanctification is progressive and increasing. One settles our status and secures our adoption. The other is God's dealing with inborn sin, starting to train us in godliness. Justification is God's declaration *for* us; this is valid for eternity and can neither grow nor decline. Sanctification is His work *within* us, which develops in time as we go on with Him. In these respects it is similar to human adoption. The legal proceedings establish that the child belongs to its adoptive parents. From that point they begin to bring the child up. They feel and clothe and love him. They rebuke and encourage, guide and instruct. Adoption without that home-love would be cruelty. God adopts us so that He may bring us up in His family likeness, so that people will look at us and give glory to Him (Mt. 5 :16).

A fifth way to look at the link lies in Christ's teaching about the new birth. The Spirit gives us new life so that we can see and trust God for our justification and submit to His Kingship. The life He gives goes on in sanctification, which is simply that life growing up from spiritual infancy to maturity.

Not in isolation

Justification does not stand in isolation. God does not justify us so that we can say, 'Right, I am saved. Now I don't need to bother with what God wants any more.' Roman Catholicism has traditionally accused Protestantism of that attitude, alleging that it is the inevitable consequence of 'justification by faith alone'. But this overlooks two facts : first, God links justification and adoption. We are not merely acquitted of guilt, but also made children of God. We come into living union with God as our Father and we love Him. We are in His family and therefore delight to do what pleases Him. Secondly, God justifies and adopts in order to sanctify; and so sanctification does not stand on its own either.

This needs emphasis because some teach otherwise. Some who reject the Bible's teaching on God's wrath and the need for atonement say that the crucial thing is a change *in us* to a new commitment or a new devotion. We need not be concerned whether salvation has an objective basis, because what matters is not pardon for guilt but our subjective experience or spiritual wholeness. This view really says that our sanctification justifies us, that our acceptance depends on our inward state. That, however, is impossible, for sanctification can never stand alone. Only the person who has been justified is in God's family and only he can begin to grow like Christ in character. That person alone will truly love and obey Christ.

This brings us to the connection between justification and doing good. It is plain that no-one can win acceptance with

God through trying to keep the law, but here the issue is different : it concerns how the justified person should live. The Bible's answer is crystal clear. When Paul was writing to Titus about 'having been justified by grace' and becoming 'heirs having the hope of eternal life', he went on : 'I want you to stress these things, so that those who have trusted in God' (*i.e.* the justified) 'may be careful to devote themselves to doing what is good. These things are excellent and profitable for everyone' (Tit. 3 :7, 8). Jesus said, 'If you love me, you will do what I command' (Jn. 14 :15). The faith that justifies leads to a life of obedience. It could not be otherwise, for where there is no obedience, there is no faith. What kind of trust in a Person is it that can ignore His will?

Put like that, the connection between 'trust' and 'obey' seems straightforward enough, until we come to what James wrote. The problem is that James seems to contradict Paul. 'A man is justified by faith apart from observing the law' says Paul (Rom. 3 :28). James affirms : 'A person is justified by what he does and not by faith alone' (Jas. 2 :24). They appear to be set on a theological collision course.

What James is getting at
James is certainly writing about faith and works : 'What good is it . . . if a man claims to have faith but has no deeds?' (2 :14). Actually the surrounding verses make his purpose clear and show what truths he is emphasizing. He knows well enough that no-one can earn salvation by works, for just a few verses earlier he wrote : 'whoever keeps the whole law, and yet stumbles at just one point, is guilty of breaking all of it' (2 :10). There is no way for even the near-perfect to gain justification by works. Having said that, he does not go back on it a few lines later. His concern is the practical one that his readers should do what the word says, and 'not merely listen to it'. If you are mere hearers, he says, you 'deceive yourselves' (1 :22). Those who hear God's Word can be under an illusion about their true condition. The problem he is looking at is not 'How can a man be justified?', but rather, 'How may we know true faith from false?' How

may we be sure we are not kidding ourselves? This, he says, is where what *shows* is so crucial.

'Show me your faith without deeds,' he challenges, 'and I will show you my faith by what I do' (2 : 18). What shows in a life indicates whether there is true faith or not. One of two things will show in anyone who claims to be a Christian. The first possibility is this : people will notice that a man 'claims to have faith' (2 : 14). He professes to be a Christian. People do not see true holiness or Christ-like love in him. In fact he is not markedly different from respectable people who make no Christian claims. Yet he does say he believes. Now that faith is not trust in God at all – it is mere intellectual assent. In that sense the devils are also believers; that is, they agree that there is one God. They even shudder at the thought, but they do not trust in Him.

You cannot be Christ's and keep your lips sealed about Him. But, says James, your lips can claim to be Christian when your heart has no saving trust in Him. James's point is that a 'say-so' never delivers the good works. Such a religion is only on the tongue and has no roots in the whole personality. It is devoid of godly living and obedience. It is on the lips only, not in the heart. That is never good enough, for James knew that only the 'word planted in you' can save (1 : 21).

The second possibility is that good works will show. This is why James cites Abraham here. 'You see that his faith and his actions were working together' (2 : 22); what strikes you about him is his obedience. He left Ur, he went to Canaan, he offered up Isaac. He lived for God; his faith was an active, working faith. James brings Rahab in for the same reason. She did good in bravely receiving the Israelite messengers into Jericho. What these people *did* showed that their faith was alive and well.

James therefore is listening to people's words and looking at their behaviour. He sees this great contrast : empty words on the one hand, active obedience on the other. He concludes that the first was only a profession of religion, whereas the second was living trust in God. Abraham did not merely agree that God is one; he trusted and obeyed. Rahab did not merely say she accepted the Israelites' religion; she acted specifically 'by faith' (Heb. 11 :31). Paul's conclusion was : we cannot earn justification, since works before faith are useless. James accepts that and goes on to give his conclusion. It is simple and practical : we can tell who is justified on Christ's principle that 'by their fruit you will recognize them' (Mt. 7 :16).

Dead and alive
If in late winter or early spring you look at two apple trees, one dead, the other alive, they look very similar. Each owner believes that his tree is alive. How can you tell? You cannot examine the roots, you can only listen to what the owners say. The man with the dead tree asserts that his is alive, but can produce no supporting evidence. The other man talks differently : 'I can show you that my tree is alive – look at the tiny buds forming already.' Later he will be able to show leaves, blossom and then fruit. These manifest the life within. But when there is nothing to be seen, the roots are suspect.

This is one of the reasons why works *after* justification matter; they demonstrate that the root of justifying faith is there. So James said that 'a person is justified by what he does and not by faith alone', that is, his justified state shows in his active obedience to God and not in his merely *saying* he believes. A life devoid of obedience has no trust in God. There is no fruit, because there is no root. A life of doing good is the fruit which springs from trust, its root.

Justified by works
It is in this sense that a man is justified by works. Good works are the result of justifying faith, for such faith and works are interlocking. Where faith is present, works are present also, and vice versa. Abraham offered Isaac; there was a work of obedience : it was his faith working. Paul would agree with this, for he wrote that the gospel was revealed so that people might 'believe and obey' God (Rom. 16 :26). Paul was glad that the Roman Christians 'wholeheartedly obeyed' (Rom. 6 :17). Peter spoke of 'obeying the truth'
66

(1 Pet. 1 :22). In the second half of many New Testament letters the readers are urged to practise their faith : 'in view of God's mercy . . . offer yourselves' (Rom. 12 :1). That is the emphasis of James also. 'Works of law' can contribute nothing to justification; but works of grateful obedience are central in the Christian life.

Faith unites us to God : the God of grace and holiness, the God of the cross and the Ten Commandments. Because we are united to Him, His will becomes ours. 'I delight to do thy will, O my God' (Ps. 40 :8). If we think or act otherwise, we have never understood God or justification. A husband who is full of the fine words of love, but never helps his wife with the washing-up, is a hypocrite. Good works express what is really in the heart. Without them trust and love are empty sentiments.

Judged by works

James and Paul agree then that true faith is active for God. This ties up with the Bible's consistent teaching that we shall be judged by works. Paul says so : 'We must all appear before the judgment seat of Christ, that each one may receive what is due him for the things done while in the body, whether good or bad' (2 Cor. 5 :10). God 'will give to each person according to what he has done' (Rom. 2 :6). Jesus said so : 'Not everyone who *says* to me, "Lord, Lord," will enter the kingdom of heaven, but only he who *does* the will of my Father' (Mt. 7 :21). The king will say to some, 'Come, you who are blessed by my Father; take your inheritance . . . Whatever you did for one of the least of these brothers of mine, you did for me.' To others he will say, 'Depart from me, you who are cursed.' Why? 'Whatever you did not do for one of the least of these, you did not do for me.' (See Mt. 25 :31–46.)

Once again we seem to have a contradiction; justified by grace but judged by works. Salvation is not by our merit, yet is affected by our deeds. It looks as though God suddenly climbs down and reverses His earlier verdict. And if God reintroduces works as the test, then we are all sunk. We came to Christ confessing that our works were useless and believed that God accepted us apart from our deeds. Yet here is God at the last day dealing with everyone according to works. It seems to undermine grace entirely.

To make it worse, all men (believers as well as un-believers) will be judged by works. We could understand this applying to non-Christians. They have not believed, so they have never claimed grace. They opted to stand on their own feet and that is justice for them. Believers, on the other hand, came to depend on Christ, so surely they should be judged differently – if at all. Yet Christ makes it plain that the blessed and the cursed go their separate ways in the judgment because of what they did. It is the works of both groups that He will examine and reward (Mt. 5:12; 24:45-51; 25:21; 1 Cor. 3:14, 15).

Rewards

As soon as rewards are mentioned, we need to speak care-fully. In everyday use 'reward' often has overtones of greed ('I want it for myself') or competitiveness ('I don't want anyone else to get it'). Needless to say, it does not have such associations in the Bible. In fact, even on the human level it can have an honourable meaning. The local paper carries the story of Mr Smith and begins : 'His forty years' devoted service to the hospital were rewarded by a retirement gift.' Through the years Mr Smith knew of others similarly re-warded on reaching 65, but he certainly did not work for forty years just to get that reward. If money had been his motive, he would have shifted jobs long before in order to make more money faster. Each day he had set his mind to the work in hand. His efforts had not been faultless, but they had been diligent and faithful and it was right that good work should be recognized. But the fact of a reward did not make the whole procedure selfish.

When the Bible speaks of rewards it is simply putting before us certain facts of spiritual life. First, rewards will be of either blessing or punishment. Thus they underline the holy character of God. He always loves righteousness and hates evil, even – perhaps especially – in His children. Grace does not cancel out this fact. It is right that at the last God should take account of our actions and this is the thought behind His testing 'the quality of each man's work' (1 Cor. 3:13).

Secondly, rewards emphasize our responsibility. God has given us time, talents, gifts, opportunities and personalities. It would be wrong if we were not accountable to God for what we do with them. It would also be wrong if God dealt identically with an idle Christian and a devoted one. After all, He gave the gifts to be used responsibly, not frittered away. He gave them in love and is concerned about how we use them. This does not mean that the believer's status as a child of God will be put in doubt : as Paul said, 'he himself will be saved' (1 Cor. 3:15). The sins which Christ put away on the cross will not be punished again. But the Father does emphasize His children's responsibility and shows how much their actions matter to Him.

Thirdly, any virtue in our good works is due entirely to God. The Christian prays as Augustine did : 'Do not despise the work of your hands; see in me your work, not mine. For if you see mine, you will condemn it. If you see your own, you will crown it. For whatever good works are mine are from you.'[1] Those who truly trust Christ will be doing such good deeds. They will not come to God with a long list of them, saying 'Look what I have done'. They will not boast of them. They will not keep a tally of them or even be conscious of them. It will pleasantly surprise them at the last day to hear the king say, 'Come, . . . take your inheritance . . . you gave . . . clothed . . . looked after . . . came to visit. . . .' They will say, 'Lord, when did we . . .?' (Mt. 25:34–37). Their whole life will have borne fruit. Good works prove the reality of faith and the transforming power of grace.

Fourthly, God gives us encouragement by His teaching on rewards. When Christ spoke to His disciples about persecution, He said, 'Rejoice and be glad, because great is your reward in heaven' (Mt. 5·12). His talk of rewards puts

[1] Augustine, *Psalms* (Ps. 138).

present troubles in a different light and leads us to have increased joy and hope in Him.

Fifthly, the Christian's great reward is God Himself. Despite this, some say the very idea of rewards is immoral. Rewards encourage selfishness, whereas the Christian should do good purely for the sake of doing good and not for what he hopes to get out of it. So do rewards mean selfishness? And what is the Christian's incentive to do good?

Certainly the believer does not live to feather his own nest in heaven. If that is anyone's chief motive, it is doubtful if he or she has really come to God. The Spirit pours out God's love into our hearts (Rom. 5 :5), not selfishness with a spiritual veneer. At the same time there is such a thing as a proper incentive for the Christian. He does not do good for the sake of some impersonal, abstract notion of goodness : He acts for God. And that ultimately brings the reward of knowing Him as fully as He now knows us.

Speculation

There is, of course, no limit to possible speculation about rewards. Will heaven be less than heaven for the less rewarded? Will some be nearer to God and enjoy Him more? The Bible cuts right through speculation and repeatedly makes one basic assertion : that God Himself is the supreme blessing and our greatest reward. 'God himself will be with them' said a voice from heaven out of the new Jerusalem (Rev. 21 :3). 'The Lamb at the centre . . . will be their shepherd' (Rev. 7 :17). This is what the believer desires; this is essentially the reward he seeks. Paul was ambitious for this, that 'I want to know Christ . . . and so, somehow, to attain to the resurrection from the dead' (Phil. 3 :10, 11). The 'crown of righteousness, which the Lord, the righteous Judge, will award' is not for those who are status-seekers in heaven, but for those who 'have longed for his appearing' (2 Tim. 4 :8). What Christian does not and should not want that? There is nothing wrong in aspiring to all that God holds out to us, for that means desiring God Himself.

Not wages but inheritance

It is not because their works are perfect that believers are rewarded, for at no stage in this life is this so. Our works do not and cannot procure us merit. That would suggest the preposterous idea that we could claim payment from God for our efforts. We cannot put in a claim for our productivity rate for alleged good works. 'The kingdom of heaven is not servants' wages, but sons' inheritance.'[2] Nevertheless, there is still a connection between works and reward. This is, as Calvin said, because God wants to 'relieve the weakness of our flesh by some comfort but not to puff up our hearts with vainglory'.[3]

This emphasis on works does not mean that God neglects the state of our hearts. Christ said, 'Out of the overflow of the heart the mouth speaks. The good man brings things out of the good stored up in him, and the evil man brings evil things out of the evil stored up in him' (Mt. 12:34, 35). Even we can often tell the motive behind the deed. Take a senior citizen, crippled by arthritis and confined to her council flat. Two people visit and help her each week. Outwardly what they do is the same : getting in the coal, cooking a meal, etc. One does it in a humble, self-effacing way, obviously concerned for the pensioner. The other is ostentatious, conscious of doing good and anxious to let everyone know it. They perform the same deeds but have totally different hearts – and the old lady notices the difference. She remembers one in these terms : 'It was nice of her to call : she *did* cheer me up.' Of the other she says : 'Well, she cooked a nice meal, but she's always on about the important people she knows. And so stuck-up !' She exemplifies what C. S. Lewis wrote : 'nothing gives one a more spuriously good conscience than keeping rules, even if there has been a total absence of all real charity and faith.'[4]

[2] J. Calvin, *Institutes of the Christian Religion*, III.xviii.2.
[3] *Ibid.*, III.xviii.4.
[4] From an unpublished letter; cited in Clyde S. Kilby (ed.), *A Mind Awake, An Anthology of C. S. Lewis* (Geoffrey Bles, 1968), p. 141.

Grace

Judgment by works simply means that God sees our works and what they spring from : faith and love to God or self-trust and self-love. He wants good-hearted, God-hearted works. Judgment on this basis does not cancel grace. Rather, it throws it into relief by displaying the difference grace makes. The transforming power of grace is so great that at the last day one simple test will be enough : 'did you *do* My will?' That will expose whether grace was present. God will not have to investigate opinions or claims. He will not need to know whether we had Christian parents, were church members or could recite the creed. Grace is so potent and trust so active that the difference they make will be obvious. Works will show this difference.

Subversive

Two main objections are levelled against this Bible teaching. Some say the whole teaching about free justification is wrong. If grace rules out our works, it is morally subversive. It kills any incentive to please God. Grace therefore must go – we must return to works as the way to gain acceptance. Only if we are unsure of heaven will we have the incentive to work for it. But the only incentive that this teaching gives is purely self-centred, for works are the attempt to make ourselves pleasing to God. Any good we do for others is, by definition, for our own sake. That may make us active, but it also makes it impossible to do anything purely for God.

Team sports offer a partial analogy. If I am trying to earn my place in the team, I am chiefly concerned about my own ability and form. In large measure I am playing for myself. 'Will I be picked again? How can I earn selection?' If, by contrast, I am assured of my place in the team, I can forget myself. I am free to give my whole effort to the club. I am not worrying whether the manager sees all my fancy skills. I don't have to score all the goals myself. 'How is the side doing?' – that is my concern.

So with a justified individual. For the first time in his life he can begin to be selfless. He is assured of his place (not on ability, as a footballer, but by grace). He can give all his energies to God and others, and so the good deeds begin to flow. He needs to apply himself (Tit. 3 :8), lest he becomes weary in doing good (Gal. 6 :9). Yet in his actions he is beginning to express gratitude instead of self-seeking. Works to earn his place are out; works to say 'thank you' for his place are in.

Licence

Others say that free justification is great. Grace is displayed in God's forgiving sin. With no sin, no grace would be seen. So we can go on sinning : not, of course, to indulge ourselves, but to let grace shine the more. The law has been abolished and we need not keep that. Pardoning grace is the key. Thus with one hand God gives us an admission ticket to heaven, with the other a licence to sin.

This is rather like a child with a magic drawing-board. He scribbles all over it. Mother slides the board up and down in its case and the scribbles are gone ! 'This is fun,' thinks junior, and scribbles some more. Mother clears the board ... more scribbles ... this can go on endlessly.

Now grace certainly does wipe the slate clean. Yet grace is not displayed so much in repeatedly wiping away our deliberate sins as in changing our life (Rom. 6 :4). God does not adopt us so that we can go on displeasing the One who is now our Father. He sets us free from sin to bring us into the glorious liberty of the children of God. This is not licence to sin, but freedom to love and follow God. Before justification we were never free, except to sin.

A child who stays at the stage of endless scribbles is not free either. He is making no progress and is probably bored as well. That is, moreover, a poor advertisement for his teacher or parents. Good parents want their child to develop from scribbles to drawings worth keeping. Similarly God gives us grace to make us creative artists in behaviour. The initiative of love and gratitude creates good works which have an eternal significance. 'You did not choose me,' Christ said, 'but I chose you to go and bear fruit – fruit that will last' (Jn. 15 :16). Such works please God, display grace and endure in the judgment. The Christian therefore says, 'I shall walk at liberty, for I have sought thy precepts . . . I find my delight in thy commandments, which I love' (Ps. 119:45, 47).

Growth

Justification leads to growth. If God has justified us, He is committed to taking us forward in grace; and we are committed to going on with God in obedience. If we are justified, we want this, for our hearts are bursting with gratitude for all God has done. In this access and attitude we do go on, until the day when we see Him face to face. God's grace and God's glory – these motives make us practise obedience and enjoy our service.

But God gives us not only access and incentive; He gives us much more besides.

8 Being sure

God gives assurance to those He justifies. Assurance is more than *access*. Every believer has access to God, because Christ died; but some believers do not enjoy that access because they feel unsure about their relationship to Him. Assurance is more than *incentive*. The motivation to live for God's glory is plain to all believers, but some do not live up to it because they are hesitant about whether God has accepted them. Assurance of salvation gives a security and stability that fires us to give all our energies to pleasing God.

Not everyone sees it like that. Many simply dismiss assurance as presumption. Many liberal thinkers have a theology of doubt which makes uncertainty an integral part of faith. If anyone is sure of God, they say, then he cannot understand very much. If he knew all the problems – philosophical, textual, moral, scientific – he would not be so certain. Roman Catholicism not only plays down assurance; traditionally it has denied it. In its view a claim to be assured of salvation is a claim to be holy enough for God. 'No one ought to be so presumptuous . . . as to decide with certainty that he is definitely among the number of the predestined.'[1] Non-Christians obviously do not know this assurance; the most they can do is vaguely hope for the best. And such talk even hoodwinks some true believers who feel (rightly) that they do not want to claim too much for themselves. It cons them into thinking that only proud people claim assurance and that the way of humility is to be a little in doubt.

[1] Council of Trent, chapter 12 (J. F. Clarkson *et al.* (eds.), *The Church Teaches*, p. 238).

75

Is assurance possible?

We must therefore ask first : is assurance possible? That sounds a fair question, but really it misses the point altogether. James Denney once said that whereas in Romanism assurance is a *sin* and in much of Protestantism a *duty*, in the New Testament it was simply a *fact*. Assurance was not merely possible, but actual. It was no hypothetical question but a living experience. Dip into the New Testament and you find assurance everywhere : 'I *know* whom I have believed . . . in full *assurance* of faith . . . faith is *being sure* of what we hope for . . . we *shall* see him as he is . . . (nothing) will be able to separate us from the love of God that is in Christ Jesus . . . Rejoice that your names *are* recorded in heaven . . . he who began a good work in you *will* carry it on to completion' (2 Tim. 1 :12; Heb. 10 :22; 11 :1; 1 Jn. 3 :2; Rom. 8 :39; Lk. 10 :20; Phil. 1 :6).

J. C. Ryle gave a beautiful, brief description of assurance. He wrote that a true Christian may reach such a comforting degree of faith in Christ 'that in general he shall feel entirely confident as to the pardon and safety of his soul – shall seldom be troubled with doubts – seldom be distracted with fears – seldom be distressed by anxious questionings – and, in short, though vexed by many an inward conflict with sin, shall look forward to death without trembling, and to judgment without dismay'.[2]

Four plain facts

It is justification that creates such assurance. That is why (and this is vital to note) those who question assurance also question justification. Such questioning overlooks at least four plain facts.

First, God cannot deny Himself by going back on His own verdict, which is based on the perfect work of His Son and backed by His Word that cannot be revoked. Secondly, God cannot and does not judge the same sin twice. If Christ has answered for it, God will not bring it against the justified sinner. 'It is God who justifies. Who is he that condemns?' (Rom. 8 :33, 34). Thirdly, justification is not an interim ver-

[2] J. C. Ryle, *Holiness* (1879; reissued James Clarke, 1956), p. 103.

dict which then depends on how much we improve ourselves. It is God's final verdict, His sentence of the judgment day brought into the now. Added to all this is the fourth fact, that Christ's honour is at stake in this matter. He said, 'This is the will of him who sent me, that I shall lose none of all that he has given me, but raise them up at the last day' (Jn. 6:39). If any were lost, that would reflect badly on Christ. The devil could then say, 'The Father gave them to Christ, but Christ could not keep them; I snatched them from Him.' Christ, however, gives His glory to no-one else. He has staked His reputation on getting every believer to glory (Jn. 6:40). If this is so, it is gross understatement to say merely that assurance is possible.

The fact that we now have God as our Father further emphasizes the solid basis of assurance. He is on record as saying that our family bond with Him is for ever: 'those he justified, he also glorified' (Rom. 8:30). Even good human parents do not throw their children out. How much more will the perfect heavenly Father care for His own. He has purposed that His Son shall be 'the first-born among many brothers' (Rom. 8:29); He will not leave His Son bereft of a single one of these brethren.

Of course, this does not mean that all who *claim* assurance are secure. In practice it is sometimes hard to see whether faith is true or spurious. A true believer backsliding may give much the same outward impression as a non-Christian who takes a temporary interest in religion. What is clear is that those who are justified are secure for ever. Assurance is more than a possibility; it is the normal, though not invariable, experience of the Christian. The prevailing picture in the New Testament is of believers assured of salvation and filled with the hope of glory.

Is assurance presumption?

But is it presumptuous to claim assurance of salvation? Not according to the references already given. Yet the view persists and we need to look at it a little more. Certainly there are presumptuous people. Some will say to Christ at the judgment day: 'Lord, Lord, did we not ... in your name ...

perform many miracles?' (Mt. 7 : 22). They had called Him
Lord, they had in some sense been involved in the spiritual
realm (even casting out demons) and were sure they had
done enough to qualify. Christ will disagree and say, 'I never
knew you. Away from me!' We all meet people who have
not the slightest doubt (apparently) that they are in with
God. Ask them why and one will say something like this :
'I've been a member of this church for fifty years and an
officer for forty-five.' Another : 'I run the YPF, and I'm in
a witness team.' A third : 'I go hospital visiting and give to
charity.' Those are the grounds of their confidence; on their
own they amount to presumption.

We need to beware of false assurance. To say 'Peace,
peace' when there is no peace (Je. 6 : 14) is the devil's deceit.
The Pharisee in the Temple trusted in himself that he was
righteous; he presumed he was good enough. The tax-
collector did not dare to thrust himself forward; no presumption, just casting himself on God. He was the one who was
accepted (Lk. 18 : 14).

Another kind of presumption occurs, though it is not so
often recognized . It is the attitude which denies assurance.
This is presumptuous because it rejects what God has said
If I deny the connection God has established between faith,
salvation and assurance, I am making myself wiser than
God. And that is pride. Humble minds accept what He has
done and said. It is not presumption to believe that the
general truth of assurance applies to me in particular.

One factor which confirms this is that when God works in
a life He leaves tell-tale marks of His presence. 'The old
has gone, the new has come!' (2 Cor. 5 : 17). Those who
think assurance is presumption must explain how the omni-
potent God can come to live in the people He has justified
without making an obvious difference. A person cannot be
'a temple of the Holy Spirit' (1 Cor. 6 : 19) without having
some awareness of the Occupant. God's presence will bring
the inward consciousness that He is, as He put it to Abraham,
'God *to you*' (Gn. 17 : 7). There will be a double confirmation
of this : the *signs* of God's presence (a new use of our time,

78

money, tongue, Bible, *etc.*) and the *sense* of it. God's Spirit confirms to ours that we are God's children (Rom. 8 :16). He gives us a sense of wonder, love and praise.

This means far more than simply drawing an inference about ourselves from a Bible verse. This view of assurance sometimes comes out in counsel given to someone who has just professed faith : 'You have trusted in Jesus? That's great. Now the Bible says that "whoever puts his faith in the Son has eternal life" (Jn. 3 :36). So you have eternal life; you have assurance; it says so. Don't worry if you don't feel any different!' John 3 :36 is certainly a wonderful verse, but if assurance is only on paper – even, be it said, the paper of the Word of God – there is something strange. It is as though a newly-married couple merely look to their marriage certificate for assurance that 'it has really happened'. The document is vital, but it would be very odd indeed if they were not vibrantly alive to each other. Feelings without the certificate could deceive. The certificate without the new awareness would not promise much of a marriage.

This is no argument for emotionalism, for the Bible never aims to produce a merely emotional response. By contrast, God's Word first addresses our minds; but when God does bring us to Christ, He also brings Christ to our hearts, and that cannot leave us unaffected. To know Christ dwelling in our hearts through faith, to sense the love of Christ which transcends knowledge, that is not presumption but the privilege of children.

It is not presumptuous of God's children to come to the Lord's Table. As Isaac Watts wrote :

> 'Jesus invites His saints
>   To meet around His board ;
> There pardoned rebels sit and hold
>   Communion with their Lord.'

He invites; that is His personal word to us. He pardoned; that was His work for us. So it is not presumption to claim to know God. Assurance is presumption only if it depends on us, but it does not :

79

'When Satan tempts me to despair,
And tells me of the guilt within,
Upward I look, and see Him there
Who made an end of all my sin.'[3]

The Christian can face his past, and that in itself speaks volumes for grace; he can look into the depths of his heart; he can acknowledge his guilt and corruption and still answer the accusations of the devil. His reply is : 'All you say of *me* is true. But you must talk of *Christ*. I am not claiming any merits for myself, but I am in Christ and He is worthy. He died and answered your charges for me.' We must examine ourselves as to whether we are in Christ; but we must not fall for the lie that true assurance is presumption.

Is assurance constant?

If I truly believe, will I always feel assured? Or, to put it another way, is assurance always part of saving faith? The answer to such questions is No. Our enjoyment of Christ may vary even though our union with Him is secure. Ryle described such a 'poor believing soul' : 'he may have no full assurance of his pardon and acceptance with God. He may be troubled with fear upon fear, and doubt upon doubt. He may have many an inward question, and many an anxiety – many a struggle and many a misgiving – clouds and darkness – storm and tempest to the very end.'[4] Many factors affect our sense of assurance – here are some of them.

1. The Lord's testings : 'No discipline seems pleasant at the time, but painful' (Heb. 12 : 11). Correction is not enjoyable in itself.

2. Our physical state : poor health or tiredness or a searing headache will not make us feel assured of anything.

3. Sin : if we fondle sin in our hearts, we cannot expect to walk in the light (Ps. 66 : 18; 1 Jn. 1 : 6, 7).

4. The devil : Peter did not enjoy having Satan trying to sift him, nor Paul the messenger of Satan sent to torment him (Lk. 22 : 31; 2 Cor. 12 : 7).

[3] From the hymn 'Before the throne of God above' by Charitie Lees Bancroft (1841–1923).
[4] J. C. Ryle, *op. cit.*, p. 109.

All these factors can blot out assurance for a while, but at such times we can remember that we are not saved because we *feel* saved, or lost simply because we feel unsure. One Roman Catholic wrote of 'this characteristic (Protestant) error, the transition to justification by assurance'.[5] The Bible and true Protestantism never put the stress there. We are saved by Christ alone, not by feelings. Faith in Him may be very hesitant, but still be saving faith : 'I do believe; help me overcome my unbelief!' (Mk. 9 :24).

'Bare simple faith shall save a man, though he may never attain to assurance; but I will not engage it shall bring him to heaven with strong and abounding consolations. I will engage it shall land him safe in harbour; but I will not engage he shall enter that harbour in full sail, confident and rejoicing. I shall not be surprised if he reaches his desired haven weather-beaten and tempest-tossed, scarcely realizing his own safety, till he opens his eyes in glory . . . Faith, let us remember, is the root, and assurance the flower Doubtless you can never have the flower without the root; but it is no less certain you may have the root and not the flower.'[6]

Self-examination

The practical question concerns what we should do when assurance is not constant. Obviously we should examine ourselves (2 Cor. 13 :5). But there is a right and a wrong way to do this, and a right and a wrong time. The wrong way is to look first for feelings; the right way is to face certain questions. Do I disclaim any merit of my own before God? Do I depend wholly on Christ and His blood shed for me? Is that the basis of my standing before God? Am I ready, on that basis, to die and meet him?

The wrong time to examine ourselves is when we are really feeling down. At such times we have a jaundiced view of life and of ourselves. 'The sinful nature desires what is contrary

[5] G. H. Tavard, *Protestantism* (Faith and Fact Books : Catholic Truth in the Scientific Age, Section XIII, Vol. 137; Burns and Oates, 1959), p. 30.
[6] J. C. Ryle, *op. cit.*, p. 109.

to the Spirit' (Gal. 5 :17) and sometimes it prevails. Self-examination in that condition will often bring us to wrong conclusions. We should choose the time well, otherwise we shall needlessly give the devil opportunity to oppress us. It is a good rule not to come to final conclusions about ourselves when we are low. As to the right time, Paul tells us specifically to examine ourselves before we come to the Lord's Supper. He does not mean that this is the only time for self-examination, but when we do it, then it leads us immediately into remembering Christ and His death. We are not left floundering in endless introspection, but turned back to Christ. He is the way back to assurance.

Our experience of assurance may vary, but the fact that God is our Father remains constant. A disobedient child will get a frown from the father who loves him. Persistent rebellion will call for action and the child at that point will not enjoy his father's love. At worst, he may become sulky; at best, contrite. Yet his father still loves him. At such moments a good human father is very concerned to assure the child of his love. He wants him to feel wanted and secure. He longs to show that his love does not end when the child misbehaves. If the child is adopted, there may be even greater concern to give assurances of love.

Sense of belonging
God wants His adopted children to know they belong. This is why the Roman Catholic denial of assurance is so wrong. Its picture of God is so grotesque. What kind of father never says to each of his children individually, 'Daddy loves you'? We know what we think of a father who threatens to disinherit his children if they misbehave. But some Protestants also have rejected assurance in its full sense. They allow a confidence that we are accepted *now*, but not an assurance that we are God's to the end. But again, what kind of father will say, 'I love you *today*' and withhold assurance about tomorrow? God is a better father than either of these notions. He does not dangle His children on the end of a string, as though He might at any moment drop them. Rather He

says, 'I have loved you with an everlasting love; therefore I have continued my faithfulness to you' (Je. 31 :3).

This is why He gave His Spirit to lead us to talk to Him by the family term, 'Father' (Rom. 8 :15, 16). The Spirit gives direct witness to our adoption. This is more than drawing inferences either from a Bible text or from the state of our lives. The Spirit gives the inward awareness that we are God's children now. Unless they are sinning and grieving the Spirit, all true Christians normally know this assurance. It moves them to say :

> 'O why did Jesus show to me
> The beauty of His face?
> Why did He to my soul convey
> The wonders of His grace?'[7]

Seeking assurance

This is the assurance which the Bible tells us to seek : 'Be all the more eager to make your calling and election sure,' said Peter (2 Pet. 1 :10). He shows us how to do this. God, he says, has supplied all we need for life and godliness. Having faith, we are to add to it goodness, knowledge, self-control, perseverance, godliness, brotherly kindness and love. We may not rest content with our initial faith or settle down with our faults and sins. We are to grow in grace and obedience. 'If you possess these qualities in increasing measure, they will keep you from being ineffective and unproductive in your knowledge of our Lord Jesus Christ' (2 Pet. 1 :8). These features of character and mind give a firm basis for assurance of salvation from within our own experience.

John agrees with Peter. 'You know that everyone who does what is right has been born of him . . . We know that we have passed from death to life, because we love our brothers' (1 Jn. 2 :29; 3 :14). We are not first to seek assurance; but when, for example, we seek to do right and to love other Christians, then assurance increases as we go along.

Our justification depends on God's Word and Christ's

[7] Adapted from the hymn by Richard Burnham (1749–1810), minister of Grafton Street Chapel, Soho.

work. Because that Word is true and that work perfect, we may have assurance. Because the God who justifies also gives His Spirit to indwell and sanctify, as we may know Him inwardly and see evidence of His presence as we are being transformed. We should not willingly settle for less.

Nevertheless, the Christian's mind is not always full of assurance and the Bible is realistic about this fact. It shows us believers in times of spiritual dryness and acute depression. Justification helps us to assurance; does it offer any help for those other times of doubt and darkness?

eve, for walking in darkness cuts out our fellowship with
d (1 Jn. 1 :6). David lost the joy of his salvation because
had an adulterous affair with Bathsheba and murdered
r husband. He had to confess ('Against thee, thee only,
ve I sinned') and pray ('Blot out all my iniquities. Create
me a clean heart . . . Restore to me the joy of thy sal-
tion') (Ps. 51 :4, 9, 10, 12).

Where spiritual depression is due to sin, the only solution
to confess the sin and give it up. Sometimes Christians try
gloss over their sin and seek some other 'cure'. Some try
quieten a bad conscience by trying to busy themselves in
me form of Christian activity. Some pretend that their
n does not really matter and that 'anyway lots of others
re just as bad'. Some say they cannot help it because 'it's
he way I'm made'. But if sin causes depression, it is no use
rying to deal with the depression other than by dealing with
he sin. In such cases it is missing the point to say the de-
ression should not be there; we must insist that it is the sin
hat should not be there.

'Just ignore it!'

A different approach to depression recognizes that it may
come to Christians. It does not so much condemn them for
being down as say to them simply : 'Just ignore it! Grit
your teeth and carry on. Don't be occupied with your feelings. "In duty's path go on." If you once start being intro-
spective, there is no end to it. The best antidote to depression
is to get on with your work and your Christian service.'

There is truth here too. Our duty remains our duty, even
if we do not feel like doing it. Moreover, God often brings
us back to joy and radiance as we go on in obedience. The
Bible does not begin to live for us by gathering dust on a
shelf, but only as we read it. Proper self-discipline harms no-
one.

Other factors

Once again, there is sometimes more to depression than this.
It will not always go away because we refuse to answer its

9 In depression

g
G
h
h
h
i
v

i
t
t
s
s

Most Christians, if not all, go through times of d
All light and joy disappear and the sense of ela
once knew evaporates. Sometimes they have a (
struggle for assurance, not just of salvation but ev
very existence of God. His ways seem mysterious a
wrong. And to the believer in depression the sight
Christians enjoying unruffled confidence in God (
presses them the more.

Spiritual dejection leads to conflicting desires – sor
to cover up and put on a brave front; at other ti
capitulate to despair. The individual thinks it imp
that anyone else should understand or sympathize. Ma
that their inner being is the battle-ground of forces qui
side them. They seem powerless to alter events, h
spectators of a conflict they are losing. How then are
face spiritual depression in ourselves and in others?

'It should not be there!'
Some have a simple answer : 'It just should not be th
Christians should know constant joy; depression is w
and probably indicates unconfessed sin.' So we should (
fess – and then cheer up. A few hearty slaps on the k
plus a verse or two of Scripture and (in theory) we are ou
it. Now it is inappropriate to deal with all the spiritu
downcast like that. If our condition is not due to sin, i
cruel to make out that it is. A slick solution will leave a s
soul.

Yet there is more truth in this approach than many adm
In the end sin will always depress; it should certainly alwa

8

knock at the door. We need to remember other factors, which are obvious but often overlooked.

We are *physical* beings. Overwork and overplay can run us down. Neglect of God's one day in seven will affect our bodies. Pressures at home or at work, tensions with others – all affect our feelings, responses, memories. This is partly why Paul said that physical training is of some value for 'the present life' (1 Tim. 4 :8). Fitness will not get us to heaven, but unfitness may make our earthly pilgrimage that little bit harder. When we get tired, one thing leads to another. We become jaded and irritable; we say things we regret; we feel remorse and know we are not living as we should; we begin to wonder what is going wrong. Depression is on its way in, for what is largely a physical reason.

We are also *spiritual* beings. If we neglect worship, miss true biblical preaching, forget to read Scripture and stop praying, then we shall not be heading for spiritual joy. Further, we are in a spiritual conflict. The devil does not want it made public, but he is alive and active. We are fighting 'against the powers of this dark world and against the spiritual forces of evil in the heavenly realms' (Eph. 6 :12). We have an opponent always seeking to wound us and often finding us with our defences down. We also have a conflict within ourselves. Even the mature apostle wrote : 'What I want to do I do not do, but what I hate I do' (Rom. 7 :15). 'The sinful nature desires what is contrary to the Spirit' (Gal. 5 :17). Our attitude to depression must therefore never be glib. Perhaps the best way to look at it is to take a case-history.

A case-history

One man recorded his experiences for us while he was thoroughly cast down. He was a true believer, a man who knew God closely and was regularly at worship. He was a man of prayer and a leader of God's people. He had been so faithful to God that those who were against God directed their mockery against him. In Psalms 42 and 43 he tells us what factors depressed him.

1. Other people taunted him: 'Where is your God?'

(42 :3). 'You say you're a believer; well, what is your God doing for you? Why doesn't he help? Not much use to you, is he?' They did this continually. Maybe he began to feel they had a point.

2. He remembered better days : once his life had been marvellous (42 :4). He had gone with the crowd to the house of God. He had sung songs of thanksgiving and shouted for joy. In fact, he had led the procession. 'Those were the days. What great joy I had then!' But now?

3. Now he was in a different place (42 :6). Not in Jerusalem, but away up in Hermon, where the springs of the Jordan rise.

4. So he was living on memories. All God's goodness seemed in the past and that made him depressed about the future.

These same factors influence us. At work we may be respected as Christians – or mocked, or pitied. We cannot always explain God very well to others. We can look back nostalgically to great days in the Christian Union or Youth Fellowship. Many were saved then; we led some to Christ. But now perhaps it is rather different. We married and moved away. The church where we now live is smaller, less active. The minister is no-one to write home about. And we find that the bottom has dropped out of our spiritual life.

How depression showed
As we follow this man's experience in these Psalms, he tells us how his depression showed itself. He was dejected one moment, elated the next. Before him lay majestic scenery, with the cascading mountain stream rushing down nearby. But this reminded him of his own misfortune at God's hands : 'all thy waves . . . have gone over me' (42 :7). He felt he was going under for the last time, until suddenly he remembered that 'the Lord commands his steadfast love' (42 :8). Then he could even sing and pray. His moods fluctuated constantly up and down.

He thought God had forgotten him and he said as much to God. He felt alone and could not fathom God's ways. In a better frame of mind he would have been content just to trust; but now he must know why (42 :9).

He kept coming back to the same questions. Others said, 'Where is your God?' He returned to this, only now it felt worse. It was as 'a deadly wound in my body' (42 :10). His opponents taunted him. Whether they increased their jeers we do not know, but to the psalmist it seemed like it.

He was preoccupied with himself and his depression. He talked to himself, full of self-pity. Basically he did want, even long for, God. Right now he could think only of himself. 'O my soul,' he wailed, commiserating with himself twice over.

We sometimes show the same signs. Up and down as Christians. The mountain top, then the valley. God seeming remote and forgetful. The same old questions chasing their tails in our heads. No interest in anyone else. Our sense of proportion goes and all our problems are magnified. For the psalmist, as for many believers today, these were symptoms of uncertainty about God. Yet this man came through. What we have said about him so far is not the complete picture. There are two other factors.

Contact with truth

First, he had not totally lost contact with God's truth. Despite his depression, indeed almost without knowing it, he still wanted to enjoy access to God, to behold the face of God (42 :2). No unbeliever wants that. He still talked as though somehow he would come to praise God again. Even when he was accusing God of forgetting him, he still called God '*my* rock' (42 :9). At first these may have been phrases repeated out of habit. After all, why shouldn't he stop believing? Why not join those who laughed at God? Somehow he could not do that. He could not follow through the logic of such thoughts because deep down he knew God as 'the God of my life' (42 :8). God forgetting him – yet God *his* God; that was a contradiction, but it brought him through. Part of him wanted to drop God, but he could not do that with his whole heart. Another voice was speaking, that of God's truth in his own experience. That kept his head above water.

Where had he found this knowledge of God? He had discovered it before in the better days. He had learnt it when he went to worship. There he had absorbed the law of the Lord. He had meditated and prayed. In those days he had never thought that this would support him in depression. He probably never thought about depression at all. Now, however, all this came to his rescue. It reminded him that his only hope was in God. He knew he could not pull himself together and that made him look again to God.

Back to basics
Secondly, what really brought him through was this : he went back to the basics. He prayed : 'Oh send out thy light and thy truth' (43 :3). He was in darkness, so he prayed the right prayer : for light. He was in ignorance, so he prayed for truth. This led him to the basic matter of his access to God : 'Let them bring me to thy holy hill and to thy dwelling! Then I will go to the altar of God' (43 :3, 4). That is an Old Testament way of speaking about justification – the sinner's access to God through sacrifice. This is crucial in depression, for when we lack the peace *of* God, we should turn to our peace *with* God. The psalmist was not now harking back to past experiences, but going back to the fact and basis of his acceptance.

He knew that he could go to God only in God's way, but he could go! God had led him and made the way open. This was more important than his enemies' oppression or taunts. He does not give a treatise here on justification and sacrifice, but his whole thought is of his admission to God. Obviously this did not answer all the questions, for mocking still came his way and circumstances were still tough; but the foundation was secure. This led him through to talk of 'God my exceeding joy' (43 :4). He rejoiced, not that life was made easy, but that once again God was everything to him.

After this he could look back on his dejection. This, I believe, was what he was doing when he asked for the third time, 'Why are you cast down, O my soul?' (43 :5). He was reviewing what he had been through. Almost in amazement, he recalled that he was depressed. He was now talking to himself in a helpful way : ' "Why are you depressed?" That's what I *was* saying. But I'm not there now. I've seen the access God has given me to Himself through sacrifice. Now I can truly hope in God. I *shall* again praise Him, my help and my God.' He was not giving a ready-made technique for coming out of the depths, for there are no push-button solutions. But his experience gives us the basic affirmation that justification is relevant to depression.

Around, in and up

When we are down we can look *around* (at others and at circumstances) and *in* (at ourselves). Those prospects are generally gloomy. Justification helps us to look *up* to God. It lifts us 'from the desolate pit' and sets our feet 'upon the rock' (Ps. 40 :2). When we cry out from the depths, it reminds us that 'there is forgiveness with thee . . . and . . . plenteous redemption' (Ps. 130 :4, 7).

You may have visited old people who were going through a time of depression, illness or bereavement. If they are Christians, you probably found one of two attitudes. Some such folk, though deeply saddened or in great pain, have a mental and spiritual stability. The winds beat on them hard, yet they do not quite keel over. They can recall words of Scripture, or, if they are too weak to say much, their faces show that they love God's truth. They unconsciously give the impression of being held. If they talk, it is about the Lord; you have a hard job to extract from them how they are. You come away feeling humbled and helped. Others are full of anxiety. Their talk is all of themselves. They don't know what they will do and they feel cut loose and drifting. Read the Bible with them and it does not seem to register. You come away feeling you cannot help at all.

What makes the difference? Perhaps temperament or circumstances, to some degree. More basically it is the fact that the first type had taken care to take spiritual supplies on board all the way through their lives. They fed eagerly on God's Word; they drank its milk and ate its meat. Especially they absorbed the truths brought together in justification.

The second kind had also genuinely trusted Christ. They too had been active in Christian work. The difference was that they had not bothered to be serious about the Word of God. They had been content with vague talk about being committed to Christ and living for Jesus. Now, when they needed it, they had little to lift them out of depression.

Justification is not an eraser to rub out depression on the spot. Without a proper understanding of it, however, depression deepens. We need to get such a hold on justification that in the dark day we shall find it holding us. And if it strengthens us in times of spiritual desolation, will it not also help us in all the other experiences and problems of the Christian life?

10 For all experiences

Luther 'found Christians in bondage to their works and observances; he released them by his doctrine of faith; and he left them in bondage to their feelings'. So commented John Henry Newman.[1] Was he right? Is this the effect of justification in the Christian's life?

Certainly feelings play a large part in our lives. Every experience produces them: joy or revulsion, enthusiasm or apathy. Catching the bus or washing up are trivial experiences which do not stir deep feelings. Seeking a job or taking an exam are more important and prompt stronger emotions. Other experiences – marriage, illness or a bereavement – involve our whole emotional life. The emotional strain of tough situations seems to break some Christians; they give up prayer, Bible reading, witness, and even worship. Many others do not crack, but feel they may do so. We need therefore to see whether justification helps us at this point. It would be small comfort if it secures our forgiveness only to put us at the mercy of our feelings. In fact it does fit us to meet the strains and stresses of our various experiences.

Ultimate and immediate

As we have already seen, justification assures the believer of his ultimate security. But it also gives immediate and practical help, and two points which James makes help us to see what this is. First, he shows that we cannot avoid trials. Often we would like to, but we shall 'fall among' them (see Jas. 1:2). Jesus used the same word to describe what hap-

[1] J. H. Newman, *Lectures on Justification*, p. 386.

93

pened to the man who started out for Jericho: he 'fell among' robbers (Lk. 10:30). He did not choose to; humanly speaking, it just happened. Secondly, James has a word for these trials or happenings. It is a rather neutral word, as 'experiences' is in English. It does not say whether the experiences are good or bad, and so James can use it to cover two shades of meaning. (Because it is one word in Greek for two ideas, our translators are in difficulties in these verses in James 1:2–13.) James is telling us that we can view any experience in two ways. We can take it either as a testing for our good or as a temptation for our harm (verses 3, 13). Either as a stepping-stone towards maturity or as an occasion for self-indulgence. Either as God lifting us up – a challenge; or as the devil dragging us down – a calamity.

Double potential

All our experiences have this double potential, and therefore how we react to them is very important. Taken in the right way, they develop spiritual staying-power and lead to growth. They may still be painful, but they strengthen our spiritual muscles. They make us all-round Christians, able to face the devil's attacks from any direction. It is like an athlete training for the Olympics. It hurts to get fit and he does not enjoy the agony of aching muscles and bursting lungs. But his coach has set the training-schedule so that he may win the gold medal. With that in his sights he does not give up and ask, 'Is it worth it?' He even welcomes the pain and counts it all joy because of what it is leading to.

Our problem is to see experiences in this light and this is where justification helps. It declares that God is *for us*. This confidence belongs to those He has called and justified. If He is for us and if His total power is on our side, who can be against us? He uses this power to give good gifts (Jas. 1:17). In His hand we know that even unpleasant experiences yield a good result. He gives only good. We may be sure of this basic truth, even though we do not understand the detailed whys and wherefores. If justification depended on us, we could never reach this assurance; but now we may sing with John Newton, the redeemed slave-trader:

'Since all that I meet
   Shall work for my good,
The bitter is sweet,
   The medicine food;
Though painful at present,
   'Twill cease before long;
And then, O how pleasant
   The conqueror's song!'[2]

Whatever else may be in doubt, the believer knows that his Lord's love to him is sure. 'The Lord is my light and my salvation; whom shall I fear? The Lord is the stronghold of my life; of whom shall I be afraid?' (Ps. 27 : 1).

Justification is of immediate practical help because it frees the Christian to look in all circumstances for opportunities to go on with God. He has no ground for complaining, 'Why has God sent this?'; he is convinced of God's kindness. He knows that God, having given His greatest gift, will not hold back His lesser gifts. So he asks, 'What is God teaching me through this? What can I learn through this experience?'

Temperament

When we are convinced of God's justifying grace, we shall be in a position to meet all circumstances. We shall work this out in relation to a variety of situations a little later on, but before doing that we must look at another factor – the question of temperament. The Bible shows us how to deal with sin and backsliding, to 'repent and do the things you did at first' (Rev. 2 :5). But temperament cannot be dealt with in the same way. Of course, God *can* change us. He can still make people wonder at the boldness He gives to uneducated, ordinary men (Acts 4 : 13, 31). Many Christians have grown out of shyness or worry, false modesty or pessimism as they have fed on the Word of God. However, God's purpose is not to make us all identical. Even in glory you will be yourself and I myself. Our temperaments are still different after conversion.

Some people can just switch off after the most worry-

[2] From the hymn 'Begone, unbelief' by John Newton (1725–1807).

making day and go straight to sleep. Others cannot do this, but lie awake ruminating. This happens to equally devout Christians. Bunyan was wise enough to show this in his different characters in *The Pilgrim's Progress*. Christian had an anxious crossing of the last river, Death; Hopeful had an easier, more serene one. That was not because of inferior faith, but because they were different.

We are slow to grasp this. One Christian, with an outgoing, unworrying nature, may look down on another who is more reticent and sensitive. He may wonder (or, worse, demand to know) where the second Christian's faith is. The second may punish himself by thinking he is hopelessly inferior to the other. Yet the 'robust' faith of the one and the 'feeble' faith of the other may just be reflections of temperament, not spiritual factors at all. It may well be that the 'feeble' Christian takes the Bible to heart more and at the end of the day proves to be the stronger.

We have to keep a delicate balance. We may not blame on temperament the sins for which we are responsible. We may not say, 'I can't help sinning, I'm just made that way', for God does not let temptation get too much for us (1 Cor. 10 : 13). Each person 'is tempted when, by his own evil desire, he is dragged away and enticed' (Jas. 1 : 14). Equally we are wrong to overlook differences of temperament. This means that the great truths of a justifying God will affect the experience of all Christians, but not all in the same degree or at the same rate or in the same way. We need to know ourselves; then we shall be able to see how justification helps in the practical aspects of Christian living. To this we now turn, picking out some of the many situations in which it helps.

Guidance

Justification does not tell us the name of the person we should marry or the firm we should work for. God does not spoon-feed us, as though we were mindless infants. But justification does assure us that He is already working for and guiding us. I remember attending a student conference, at which one session was allocated to 'Guidance'. We all came expecting advice on practical problems : how to know God's will, how to choose between different jobs, how to be sure our motives are pure, what if we miss God's way? The speaker began. He talked about the character of God and seemed a long time getting to the subject. He expounded on God as the Covenant God, the great Shepherd of His flock. He continued about His unlimited power and sovereign purposes. Then he stopped. It was all over and we felt cheated. We had come for practical help, not preaching or a theological discourse.

In fact we had been given the most practical help possible. On reflection we began to see that this actually solved the greatest problem about guidance. Like others, we had had two worries about this question : first, whether God could or would guide us at all; and secondly, how we should know what that guidance (if any) was. The second worry assumes enormous proportions if we are uncertain about the first; but justification settles the first. God is God and He is for us. He is not a celestial careers bureau, able to help only when we ring Him up. Our whole life is in His hands. We do not have to persuade Him to guide. He has been guiding, every minute – as our justification proves. He is guiding right now. He will guide all through. 'Your God is King, your Father reigns.'

We do not have to ask God to step in. He is in already. We need rather to ask for discernment to grasp His will and grace to do it. We may not always be able to see His way, but without doubt He has His way and is leading us in it. It is preposterous to think that He went to the length of justifying us, only to leave us to our own devices. Justification helps us in the prime problem of guidance.

Failure
Failure is hard to take in any sphere, especially for a young Christian who started out with such high hopes. Justification helps here also. It began by showing us what we were really like : defiled, dead in sin, slaves to self-love, moral failures. Failure reminds us of this and keeps us humble. It also leads us back to the nature of the God who justifies. He will not

write us off because of failure, yet sin offends and grieves Him; He will therefore deal with us in the discipline of grace. He will lead us to know and confess our sin. What He will not do is walk out on those He bought at such a price. He has said that He 'is faithful and just and will forgive us our sins and purify us from all unrighteousness' (1 Jn. 1:9) – faithful to His Word and just because He forgives on the basis of Christ's death.

Justification stabilizes us when we fall. The unbeliever does not know this and so runs away from God when he is found out, as Adam hid himself from God when he fell. Judas was filled with remorse after betraying Christ. Neither turned to God, but the believing person does. David, almost in spite of himself, was drawn back to God after his sin with Bathsheba, as Psalm 51 proves. Peter turned again after his denials. When he heard John say 'It is the Lord', he jumped out of the boat to meet his risen Lord. The faith that justifies holds God's children to Him even when they fall.

Power

We need power and, through Him who loved us, we are more than conquerors (Rom. 8:37). In Christ God always leads us in triumph (2 Cor. 2:14). With access to God we have all His resources opened to us, so that Paul can say: 'My God will meet all your needs according to his glorious riches in Christ Jesus' (Phil. 4:19). These are the assurances He gives to the justified.

The Christian does not need one set crisis-experience subsequent to justification in order to have power. He does not, as some have taught, live between Easter and Pentecost until he has some further experience. It is not a case of his having Christ as Saviour but not as Lord, for Christ cannot be so divided. The Lord may graciously give us special proofs of His love and kindness. His Spirit is free to give His children those experiences which He wills for them individually. All of them, however, are temples of the indwelling Spirit. He gives them power to grow and to know God. He helps them to increase in holiness and obedience. This is because power comes from the presence of God – and justification brings us into His presence.

In the city of Corinth some were sexually immoral, idolaters, adulterers, male prostitutes, homosexual offenders, thieves, greedy, drunkards, slanderers and swindlers. 'And that is what some of you were,' Paul wrote to the church. 'But you were washed, … sanctified, … justified in the name of the Lord Jesus Christ' (1 Cor. 6 :11). Cleansing from defilement and power over the old sins went along with justification.

Justification leads to power in another sense also. We are always subject to pressures from others, both non-Christians and fellow Christians. Even Christian work has its fads and fashions, tempting us to conform just because 'everybody's doing it'. We fear what others will say. The justified person, however, has faced God. He fears Him more than the opinions of others. Justification gives him the moral courage to stand, when necessary, against the stream. Anyone convinced that God's is the only approval that finally matters will have strength in living. Justification breeds that conviction.

Witness
We need boldness in witness and this too flows out of justification. When a person has felt God's judgment on him and then known justification through Christ, he will have something to say – and boldly. 'Judge for yourselves whether it is right in God's sight to obey you rather than God. For we cannot help speaking about what we have seen and heard' (Acts 4 :19, 20). Justification had brought the apostles into 'God's sight'. They had seen and heard *Him* and so did not fear the reactions of others.

By contrast, some testimonies go like this : 'I do rather hope that I am a Christian. I'm not very worthy, but I do my best, try to be kind and go to church.' That is the consequence of being unsure of justification. All that such a person can pass on to others is uncertainty. Without justification there can be no true witness. When we hesitate in witness we need to remember this. God is not ashamed to be called *our* God; Jesus is not ashamed to call *us* brothers (Heb. 2:11). He stood in for us before Pilate, Herod and the hatred of the Jews. For us He took on all the evil powers. He did that to justify us. With that in our minds, we shall not be deterred from speaking by the taunts or apathy of others.

Joy

Many experiences are naturally depressing. Standing in the presence of God, however, we can see more. We can rejoice in the Lord and praise Him always (Phil. 4:4). Previously we had no joy at all. Fun, kicks, excitement, pleasure – yes; but no joy. Joy is the mark of the Christian. We saw that the psalmist called God 'my exceeding joy' (Ps. 43:4). Access makes for rejoicing about the future, unutterable and exalted joy. Access helps the Christian to rejoice now, even in distress. It teaches him to count it pure joy when he falls into various trials (Jas. 1:2). It is not just that he can discern a faint glimmer of light; or that for the most part he can be cheerful. Viewed in the light of justification, even testings can be counted all joy.

Thanksgiving

This also springs from justification. Secure in God, we can give thanks always and in all circumstances (Eph. 5:20). We can give thanks even when we cannot understand, perhaps especially then. At the very least, the believer is thankful things are not worse! He knows he deserves infinitely more troubles. Whatever his situation, it is better than being without God and without hope. Justification gives him the perspective of eternity; and so he contrasts his present troubles with the glory to come. The first are for a moment, the second for ever (2 Cor. 4:17, 18). The justified know that their chief interest is secure, and can therefore be content in passing troubles.

Prayer

Justification brings us to God and teaches us to speak to Him as our Father. God the Father will not turn a deaf ear to His own Son: and we are in Christ. God hears us for

Christ's sake. This is true only of the justified, for only they may enjoy the promises the Father makes : 'Before they call I will answer, while they are yet speaking I will hear' (Is. 65 :24). We may ask and ask without fear of being cold-shouldered or reproached. God never says, 'That's your quota of requests for today' (see Jas. 1 :5b). That is how a slave would be treated; but we are now His friends, His children. So He gives generously – generous gifts in a generous spirit. He is always alert to His children's call. We can pray to the Father only because of justification.

Some well-meaning folk are always praying to Jesus. They start with Jesus and end with Jesus. They never seem to address or think of the Father. They show that they have never properly understood salvation. They forget that our chief problem was the wrath of God and that Jesus died to 'bring us to God' (1 Pet. 3 :18). The Father adopted us; that is why Christ taught us to pray to 'our Father'. The Spirit does the same (Rom. 8 :15, 16). Justification means we come to the Father through the Son. As we do so, we find that His ear is open to us.

Christian fellowship

Justification creates believers and so creates fellowship. The trouble with many churches is that they deny or ignore justification. (When did your fellowship last hear from Scripture of justification?) They thereby become mere religious clubs. Then the typical club spirit is more apparent than true sharing in Christ. This is also the trouble with schemes for reunion that hinge on questions of sacraments, ministry and church order rather than that of justifying faith. Such schemes cannot promote true fellowship. If a church neglects this truth, it must by definition overlook vast areas of the Word of God and get much out of focus. That can lead only to impoverishment.

Sometimes there are problems within a company of true believers. Some members are nervous because they feel less gifted. They cannot take the lead or give a striking testimony, so they mark themselves down in their own minds. They always take the back seat and leave the initiative to other more prominent members. These in turn look down on the first group. 'They are fringe members. They'll never accept responsibility; we have to do it all. We know we're more gifted, but why should we have to carry the whole load?'

Both attitudes injure fellowship. Suspicion or secret criticism always does. This is how it sometimes works out for a new convert: 'In the first flush of conversion, a man feels himself unreservedly welcomed into (the religious community). He has boundless admiration for the spiritual leader . . . who has revealed the truth to him. . . . The leader gives him his unreserved confidence. Our convert deserves it; indeed, he is transformed. . . . And he experiences brotherly communion.

'But little by little, disillusionment creeps in. He notices that his spiritual leader is not faultless. . . . And then in the community there are some rather unpleasant people . . . there are cliques, opposing theological tendencies, intrigues. Backbiting flourishes. . . .

'And then he begins to doubt the efficacy of grace. . . . Judgment (i.e. unfair criticism) has done its destructive work. In his church they still play the fraternal community game . . . but it is only the façade which hides innumerable repressed judgments. All the members hold one another guilty, all are crushed.'[3]

Many fellowships are gloriously free from such in-fighting. But while 'there is jealousy and quarrelling among you, are you not worldly? Are you not acting like mere men?' (1 Cor. 3:3). Such things have kept non-Christians away from the gospel; they have made some Christians leave their local fellowship and even driven some into the spiritual wilderness. The basic answer to these wrong attitudes to fellowship is in the truth of justification.

Realism
Justification tells us the truth about what is in all of us. It prepares us to be realistic: not to think that anyone is without faults or always to be followed. It deals with those who

[3] Paul Tournier, *Guilt and Grace*, pp. 100f.

are still sinful, though accepted. It prepares us to make allowances for failure. This does not mean that we lower our standards, but that we criticize ourselves first. If I can accept God's view of myself, I can accept others. Self-judgment makes for sympathy and understanding.

Justification also tells us that believers are accepted because of Christ, not because they are perfect. We are to accept and have fellowship with them for the same reason : not because we happen to like them, but because Christ died for them. It is justification that says that 'there is neither Jew nor Greek (no distinctions because of race or previous religion), slave nor free (no distinctions because of social class, wealth or education), male nor female (men and women are equally justified), for you are all one in Christ Jesus' (Gal. 3 :28).

These natural distinctions are not obliterated. Man is still masculine, woman still feminine. Effeminate men and masculine women are still unnatural. The slave is still relatively poor compared with the free. There are still differences of function within the church and various gifts and callings. But in one thing there is no difference : the fact and degree of acceptance. All are equally pardoned, equally valued, equally welcome. There are no second-class citizens in heaven. I therefore do not need to project an image; I am content to belong to God and to have and use the gifts He has given.

The fact is that we cannot have a truly communal outlook until we have been thoroughly individual with God. We go wrong with others because we do not see the truth about ourselves. We criticize because we think *we* are above criticism. Justification sets us before God and deals with these misconceptions. It separates us from the mass and makes us face our Judge, alone. It stops me comparing myself with others and makes me compare myself with Christ. Justification is personal.

It is also corporate. When I have seen myself before God, when He has delivered me from self-righteousness, then I can begin to give myself to others and to accept them, warts and all. I see them now as members of the same family, from the same sinful descent, but saved by the same grace. I see the church not as an ecclesiastical structure but as the company of fellow believers. A grasp of this truth is essential to fellowship. Moreover, the God who justified also teaches that the differences of gift and function are of His grace and no cause for criticism or envy.

Death

'We have gained access ... and we rejoice in the hope of the glory of God' (Rom. 5 : 2). Realistic hope is hard to come by. Many people have hopes : perhaps of marriage, the pools, prestige or promotion. Such hopes are often just wishful thinking; and if they come true, they do not bring happiness. Many hope against hope for the life to come, but that is just whistling in the dark to keep their spirits up. They can only 'hope' so long as they are unrealistic about death. This is why so many 'by their fear of death' are held in slavery all their lives (Heb. 2 : 15).

I remember going to the funeral of someone in his twenties who had been killed outright in a car crash. A great number of his friends attended the service, people who were achieving success in business, the professions and sport. Many were in tears in the service, tears of sorrow but maybe also of fear. Perhaps they had never before looked at death for themselves. Here it stared them in the face : instant death, so horribly final; the death of a young man – one of their number, now beyond recall. Only the justified person can be realistic about death and still have hope.

His hope is not vague or tentative, but totally certain. It is the glorious prospect of seeing God, because justification makes his eternity secure. The Christian may be apprehensive about the experience of death, for he has never been that way before. He will feel for those he is leaving behind. Like Christian in *The Pilgrim's Progress* he may feel he will go under, but he does know the outcome in advance. Christ has told him about heaven : 'I am going there to prepare a place for you ... that you also may be where I am' (Jn. 14 : 2, 3). He looks for Christ's prayer to be fulfilled to him : 'Father, I want those you have given me to be with me where

I am, and to see my glory' (Jn. 17 :24). Justification brings
that hope and because God's love has been poured out into
our hearts by the Holy Spirit, we know that our hope will be
fully realized one day (Rom. 5 :5).

11 Life together

Early in the Reformation Luther saw that it was by the truth of justification that a church would stand or fall. He was only echoing the words of the apostles. Paul, for example, had to reprove some churches on this point. 'You foolish Galatians! Who has bewitched you?' (Gal. 3 :1). Some were drifting away from Christ. To bring them back, Paul directs them straight to the truths enshrined in justification : Christ crucified and made a curse for sinners, the importance of faith, God reckoning righteousness to believers. This was the gospel. Hence his insistence that anyone, yes anyone, who preached a different message was eternally condemned (Gal. 1 :8, 9).

Luther saw this with great clarity. 'Here appears an exceeding great fervency of spirit in the apostle, that he dare curse all teachers throughout the whole world and in heaven, who pervert his gospel and teach any other : for all men must either believe that gospel that Paul preached, or else they must be accursed and condemned.'[1] Remove justification and the church begins to crumble. The buildings will stay up, maybe for years. The traditions will go on and some people will still come. Without justification, however, there is nothing left to create faith. What may once have been a company of believers degenerates into a religious club. God is long-suffering, but He does not stay indefinitely with those who reject His gospel. This is the terrible silent testimony of church buildings now used as garages, warehouses or mosques.

[1] Martin Luther, *Commentary on St Paul's Epistle to the Galatians*, on Gal. 1 :8, 9.

Justification is totally against formal religion. God has no room for those who persist in relying on forms or ceremonies. He does not even allow people to depend for salvation on the two signs Christ commanded. No-one is justified merely by going through a form of baptism or attending communion. Newman wrote that 'faith justifies because baptism has justified' and that essentially Roman Catholic idea has permeated many non-Roman circles. It is the basis of much ecumenical thinking.

Accepting baptism

This view starts by 'accepting baptism' and asserts that all the baptized are by definition Christians and are to be treated as such : the baptized *are* the church. In fact, however, if anyone bases his standing on baptism (whether of infants or adults), he is setting up a rival gospel. He is acting like a Jew who trusts in his circumcision. He is saying that, over against justification by faith, there is the way of justification by baptism : first enter the church through baptism, then you are justified. Individuals are not incorporated into the church 'because they are justified, but they participate in the collective justification because they have received membership in the community'.[2] 'Justification comes through the sacraments,' Newman said, 'and is received by faith.'[3] 'No one is justified except by the actual reception of baptism.'[4]

On this view the rite is crucial; so therefore is the body that dispenses it; and so also is a priesthood. The 'church' must administer the sacraments and bring the individual into a state of grace. The 'church' must be there to keep that person in that state. If the 'church' teaches, for example, that penance, or confession to a priest, or prayers to Mary are necessary to salvation, then so be it. The 'church' is in charge of justification and comes in effect to take the place of Christ.

Much ecumenical thinking starts by similarly 'accepting

[2] Cited in Hans Küng, *Justification*, p. 215 from *Justification* by Tobac.
[3] J. H. Newman, *Lectures on Justification*, p. 316.
[4] J. F. Clarkson *et al.* (eds.), *The Church Teaches*, p. 217.

baptism'. On this basis some in such circles are against what they call proselytism. They have objected, for example, to Evangelicals working in 'Orthodox' countries. Ethiopia provides a sad example of this. During and after the Italian invasion in 1935 (when missionaries had to leave) tens of thousands turned to Christ and young churches sprang up by the hundred. But they ran into persecution, much of it from the hostility and suspicion of the Orthodox church. A report on this conflict was prepared for the World Council of Churches, but 'the WCC declined to take action in the conflict, for the Orthodox church is a member of the Council'.[5] Such a reaction sets aside the fact that countless 'Orthodox' folk show no understanding of the gospel and no evidence of grace. Such folk are technically members of the church; they have been baptized and 'are therefore Christian'. Missionary work, we are told, should be directed to the heathen, not to the baptized.

The same type of thinking operates in allegedly Protestant circles. Go house-to-house visiting and you will soon find those who say, 'O yes, I'm a Christian; I've been christened and confirmed *and* I go to Easter Communion.' Go to some Baptist churches and ask, 'Are you a Christian?' and the answer will sometimes be, 'Of course, I've been baptized.' Go to other groups and the replies will be similar : 'Yes, didn't you know that I've been a member for forty-six years? that I'm a deacon? that I'm on the PCC? that I can speak in tongues?'

Formalism

Such formal religion crops up not only in churches which practise infant baptism, but also in those which seek to baptize believers. Indeed, some who deny infant baptism have been guilty of pressing people prematurely into 'believers' baptism' – an action that, on their own premises, is as meaningless (because without faith) as they allege infant baptism is. They have performed an empty rite and stored up trouble for the individual and the church.

Formalism is not the prerogative of any one view or

[5] F. Peter Cotterell, *Born at Midnight* (Moody Press, 1973), p. 154.

denomination, for it is part of human nature. It is so much simpler to say, 'I've been done; I'm all right. The ceremony has been held. The rite observed. All is now well.' The Jews did this throughout the Old Testament period and God constantly had to rebuke them : 'Who requires of you this trampling of my courts? . . . I cannot endure *iniquity and solemn assembly* . . . your appointed feasts my soul hates . . . Wash yourselves; make yourselves clean . . .' (see Is. 1 : 12–20). Think of the combination – iniquity and solemn assembly. Their religious acts were iniquitous because they did not spring from the knowledge and experience of God through justification – a principle that still applies.

The New Testament says the same. It never puts church membership or true worship on a formal basis. The church is not a company of the more or less indiscriminately baptized, with a remnant of believers at its heart. The New Testament does not describe the church by the 'lump and leaven' analogy : a 'lump' of nominal Christians who have been through the correct initiation rite, plus a 'leaven' of genuine Christians. The church is not 'a church within a church'. This comes out again and again as the New Testament letters address the churches. The apostles naturally and constantly refer to faith, repentance and similar gospel terms when describing the fundamental marks of the churches. This does not at all mean that baptism is unimportant, as we shall indicate. It is simply a case of first things first. Baptism is secondary in that it derives its significance from the gospel and the faith it symbolizes.

Faith and the church

Paul, Peter and John all emphasize that the local churches are bodies of genuine believers. Paul thanked God 'for all of you (at Rome), because your faith is being reported all over the world' (Rom. 1 : 8). 'The church of God' at Corinth consisted of 'those sanctified in Christ Jesus and called to be holy' (1 Cor. 1 : 2). The church at Colosse was composed of those who were 'the holy' (set apart by God for Himself) 'and faithful' (or believing) 'brothers in Christ' (Col. 1 : 2). The Thessalonians had 'turned to God from idols' (1 Thes. 1 : 9).

Peter wrote to those 'chosen according to the foreknowledge of God the Father, by the sanctifying work of the Spirit, for obedience to Jesus Christ' (1 Pet. 1 :2); to 'those who through the righteousness of our God and Saviour Jesus Christ have received a faith as precious as ours' (2 Pet. 1 :1). John said, 'I write to you, dear children, because your sins have been forgiven on account of his name' (1 Jn. 2 :12). Jude sent his letter to 'those who have been called, who are loved by God the Father and kept by Jesus Christ' (verse 1). The apostles were in no doubt about the standing of their readers – and when they were, they made that clear. When, for example, some Galatians were turning aside, Paul did not say, 'You've been baptized, you must be Christians; I appeal to you as such.' Instead he wrote : 'You . . . have been alienated from Christ; you have fallen away from grace' (Gal. 5 :4). Such people were in a totally different category from his Christian readers.

In New Testament days, therefore, not everyone associated with the churches was a true believer. Ananias and Sapphira seemed good enough members until they were found out. So did Demas, till he deserted. Jude knew that ungodly people had secretly gained admission and were denying Christ. But the churches were bodies of believers and were treated as such.

No guarantee
Obviously no-one can guarantee that a local church will consist exclusively of God's chosen people. No-one can tell, always and unerringly, who are true believers. Even the apostles could only go by what they, with the Spirit's help, could discern in people. It is always possible that the church on earth will have within it those who are not actually born again. 'Gospel hypocrites' may keep company with true saints this side of glory.

The New Testament clearly recognizes this situation. This is why James, for example, wrote about how true faith may be distinguished in practice from an empty profession of religion. It is precisely because of the danger of the church becoming a 'mixed multitude' that the New Testament does not let us resort to some form of sacrament or ceremony as the qualification for admission. Four points are relevant in this matter.

First, it is one thing to recognize that there may be gospel hypocrites in a church; it is quite another to adopt a basis for the church which actually encourages it to be a mixed multitude. To make any form of Christian initiation the test positively stimulates trust in outward forms and thus promotes nominal Christianity. The fact that we cannot guarantee a born-again membership is no excuse for lowering God's standards.

Secondly, the New Testament rules out rites and ordinances, sacraments or ceremonies as in themselves a basis for church membership. For this it points us only to living, justifying faith and says : 'That is what to look for; that is the test; that is what is vital for membership.' (See all the references from Paul, Peter and John earlier in this chapter.) There is no other way. This is not fool-proof, because we do not see men's hearts as God does. But at least it operates by reference to God's standards and gospel rather than outward ritual.

Thirdly, the New Testament does in fact give us tests by which we may know who are the children of God and who are those of the devil (1 Jn. 3 : 10). We may not be able to tell in all cases, but John encourages us to believe that, with the tests he gives, it is possible to know in most. We can judge by the wrong tests, of course. ('He can't be a believer : he does not come to our meetings . . . She must be a Christian : she's in a gospel group.') But it is also possible to work by the Bible's tests of belief, character and conduct. We are not left to anyone's mere say-so. The marks of grace are not invisible. In practice an ordinary believer who is at all grounded in Scripture will discern these marks.

Fourthly, this does not empty the sacraments of their true meaning. That happens only when they are exalted above Christ's intention and made the vehicles of salvation. Rather, the ordinances come to their full significance when they spring from grace and are seen to express living faith. Then they exhibit the justifying grace of God. Then they are genuine signs of the grace of God in an individual.

Baptism and communion

Both ordinances, baptism and the Lord's Supper, focus on the death of Christ. Baptism is a vivid picture of the death He endured; it portrays His 'going under' and His burial. It asserts by its very symbolism that He really died. The bread and wine are two distinct elements which the believer receives separately; they speak of His body being broken and His blood poured out. Baptism and communion derive their meaning from the gospel of 'Jesus Christ and him crucified'.

When rightly used, both are signs that the individual who receives them has experienced the salvation which the gospel of 'Christ crucified' brings. Baptism is the public and visible sign that the individual has entered the company which Christ created by His death – the church. It marks him as now a fellow-member with the other believers. The Lord's Supper is the unmistakable sign that the individual depends on Christ and constantly feeds on Him by faith with thanksgiving.

Baptism and communion thus seal and confirm to the Christian what is already his by grace. This is why he finds them so profoundly moving. There is nothing magical or automatic about their effects. They are not ecclesiastical slot-machines, into which you feed the right formulae and from which you receive the predetermined portion of grace. They do not yield some special kind of grace. They do not give the individual a status he did not have before. But they remind him of the One who secured his status at the cost of the cross. They are signs to him of his heavenly Father's love, confirming to him that God has accepted him in Christ. They are a sign and testimony of his personal participation in Christ who died and rose again.

In such ways these two acts which Christ commanded nourish the Christian's faith and strengthen his assurance. They are utterly different from a merely formal rite. This is why Scripture never allows that anyone is qualified simply because he has been 'done'. Justifying faith is still the working basis of fellowship in the church, still the test of admission, still the point and purpose of her life. The ground for sharing in the life of Christ's body is living faith in the Head of the church. This means a faith that holds the truth and lives it out; a trust that has doctrinal content and an effect on behaviour.

Discipline and the church

Such faith is so important for the church that the New Testament enjoins discipline for those who go contrary to it. Obviously the early church attached much importance to reproof and instruction for wayward Christians. But in certain circumstances the New Testament also urges discipline. The church must take firm action in love about basic error or serious misconduct. This action seeks first to correct and restore the individual in compassion; but if he rejects that approach, the church must deal with the individual and even remove him from the fellowship. The reason for such discipline is the good both of the individual and of the whole church.

If a church allows a member to persist in belief or behaviour that contradicts justification or the good works that should flow from it, then that church is in danger. By its 'tolerance' it is undermining the basis of its own life. If it falls away from the truths of justifying faith, it is falling away from Christ.

To ward off such necessary discipline, it is not enough for a member to produce a membership card or baptismal certificate. If he does that, he is missing the point. It is not a question of being a paid-up member of a club, but of being a responsible individual in a community of believers which bears the name of Christ. Any other basis for church life undercuts the gospel.

Vital activities undercut

When the church emphasizes rites or ceremonies as the test of admission or continuance, it undercuts three vital activities: evangelism, fellowship and worship.

1. Evangelism. By this I do not mean organized evange-

listic activity, but the evangelistic impact which the very life of a company of believers can and should have. Paul implies in 1 Corinthians 14:24, 25 that church membership should not be mixed but that church congregations should be. So, when a non-Christian comes into the church, he should become aware of two things: first, a welcome from true believers; and secondly, a sense that he does not belong – that the members have something he lacks, that he is not yet one of them in the family of God.

If the church is itself a mixture of believers and un-believers it cannot exert that power which will make the non-Christian say 'God is really among you!', will convict him of his sin and lead him to confess it.

2. True fellowship. When the church gives first place to forms, it encourages nominal Christianity; and there is a world of difference between formal adherents and genuine believers. True fellowship cannot exist on a merely formal basis. Members cannot share their experience of Christ if some have such experience and others do not. That only leads to embarrassment or divisions within a church, or even to absentee membership.

3. Worship. Formalism does nothing to discourage people from merely going through the motions. They mean well, but the great thing to them is not meeting the risen Christ among His people, but the fact that they have been in a church building and done the right thing. Only when God's justifying grace grips a person will he come with awe and wonder to worship God from the heart. But a church in which membership is based on outward rites can never unitedly engage in true worship. The whole membership needs to be 'like-minded, having the same love, being one in spirit and purpose' (Phil. 2:2). All should be able to say, 'The Lord is my light and my salvation'; then they will all seek the same thing: 'One thing have I asked of the Lord, that will I seek after; that I may dwell in the house of the Lord all the days of my life, to behold the beauty of the Lord, and to inquire in his temple' (Ps. 27:1, 4). That is a foreign language to the formal adherent.

Worship is the sum total of all our response to God as His

children. To seek guidance is to worship Him for His care, wisdom and control. To confess sin is to acknowledge His holiness. To know victory is to praise Him for His power. To witness is to tell of His saving deeds. To rejoice in the Lord is to exalt His grace. To be thankful is to record His kindnesses. To pray is to acknowledge Him as Father. To enjoy fellowship with other Christians is to thank God for creating His church. Yet worship is more than all these. Worship is to acknowledge God to be the Lord, to see and respond to all that He is. And what He is stands out most clearly in justification. His holiness and wrath, His wisdom and knowledge, His patience and care, His grace and mercy are all placarded in the truths of justification. So justification leads logically to worship. It is as Isaac Watts wrote about the cross :

> 'Here His whole name appears complete,
>   Nor wit can guess, nor reason prove,
>   Which of the letters best is writ,
>   The power, the wisdom, or the love.'

Worship and experience

Justification also leads to worship in experience. The justified person has seen something of the Lord in His beauty and glory and has been brought near. He has access and is adopted. He knows and adores the only true God. He sings with Mary, 'My soul praises' (or magnifies) 'the Lord and my spirit rejoices in God my Saviour' (Lk. 1 :46, 47). We see things bigger through a magnifying glass. The justified man sees God, not bigger than He is, but bigger than he had thought Him before. God fills his sight and other things seem smaller as God becomes all in all. That is worship : full of reverence and awe, full of intimacy and delight. And when Christians worship God *together* in this way, they have a foretaste of heaven and glory.

Revival

The church that has justification at its heart is a church that will stand. This is borne out strikingly in the history of revivals. In every period when God has awakened His people, the gospel of justification has come to the fore. The sharpness of its stress on God's holiness and man's sin has humbled men. The wonder of its stress on God's grace in the death of His Son has transformed them. To grasp this great truth will not produce revival; but we can be sure that when God again comes in His awesome power, this truth will be powerfully displayed. It must be so. This is *the* good news from Father, Son and Holy Spirit – the news which the church must make known to all people.

12 Making Christ known

In the New Testament evangelism was not an activity that could be separated off from the life and worship of the church. It was not the special preserve of the experts. It was not primarily a matter of organization or publicity or rallies. Evangelism was largely the natural by-product or overflow of the church's experience of grace.

This is why the church's life, as we were looking at it in the previous chapter, is so vital for evangelism. The church itself must be right, not for the sake of organizational efficiency or neatness and not only to conform to the divine pattern. Its message and life must be right because these can have a profound effect on those yet outside. The gospel should come to the world not from a few unattached individualists who may understandably be considered cranks with a bee in their bonnet; it is to come from people who are known to be members of Christ's body and in whose corporate life the good effects of the gospel may be seen.

Crucial for evangelism

The truths of justification are crucial within the church's life; they are equally vital when we come to consider evangelism more directly. They are the only foundation of Christian witness, though they do not always appear so from the way some evangelistic efforts are conducted. Some of these seem to say everything right – except justification. They go on their way without ever mentioning it. 'That', they imply, 'is just a doctrine. We're giving people Jesus. So it's not worth quibbling about one omission.'

That would be fine, except that it is not just one omission.

It is impossible to omit justification without omitting infinitely more, for justification holds all the aspects of the gospel in focus. Indeed it *is* the gospel : without it we have no good news to tell. Leave out justification and we leave out a great deal more than just a word. And when we forget justification, certain consequences follow : never all at once, but gradually.

The symptoms do not all come out together. They appear some here, some there. But when they do show themselves, they look like this. Sin is not mentioned and sins get only the briefest comment. The stress is on our lack of peace and purpose and satisfaction, not on offending a holy God. God is not presented as He is; everyone is assured that He is there to love them, but little is said about His holiness, wrath or judgment. The fearfulness of falling into the hands of the living God is overlooked; God is too amiable for that. Repentance is replaced by remorse or self-pity. Conviction of sin gives way to the feeling of 'what I'm missing'. The cross may be there as an unexplained sign of God's love, but its exact bearing on sin is not made plain. The new birth by God's Spirit is transposed into the need for human commitment. Assurance is related to my response more than to God's work. The Christian life is one of great activism and excitement rather than holiness of character or knowing God.

Without justification, everything becomes superficial. There is no depth, no substance, no body to the message. All is keenness and enthusiasm – precious qualities, which should not be despised; but there is little to lead people to be 'rooted and built up in him, strengthened in the faith as you were taught, and overflowing with thankfulness' (Col. 2 :7).

Extreme example
I had a vivid (and, I trust, extreme) example of this 'gospel' not so long ago. One Saturday morning a young stranger knocked on my door. 'Good morning. You're the minister? Well, God has told me I'm to preach in your church tomorrow.' This interested me, because I believed that God had also told me to preach there. I asked what he would say and he explained at some length. When he had finished, I asked :

'Is there anything you've forgotten? Is that all you'd want to say? No other truths or emphases you'd like to bring in?' He thought for a while and then said, 'No. That's the whole of it, in outline.' He had managed to talk for half an hour without mentioning, in word or concept, God's holiness or man's guilt, sin or repentance, the cross or judgment, grace or wrath. It was all Jesus, and satisfaction, and peace, and purpose, and real living, and being turned on.

Such a gospel would not be improved merely by inserting the word 'justification' into the message. It is not just that a word is important. After all, the Bible uses various words for the one basic idea. The point is that justification represents a whole perspective : God's revealed way of thinking about Himself and His Son and us.

Light and dark
Justification embraces the light and the dark shades in the gospel. God used a rainbow as a sign of His covenant with Noah after the flood, and the gospel is like the rainbow. It has its bright and glowing colours : pardon and peace and grace. It has also its darker shades : God's holiness and man's desperate state. The gospel is the whole rainbow, bright and dark together. It is possible to paint the lighter colours on their own, but the result is unrecognizable as a rainbow. It is possible to depict the brighter side of the truths about God and man, and this is what some do in evangelism. The result is unrecognizable as the full gospel, simply because justification has gone. All that is said may be true; but it is not the gospel, only some aspects separated out. It is no accident that justification disappears when certain approaches to Christian communication come in.

Some forms of communication just cannot carry the *whole* gospel. Some types of message may be very arresting : the speaker is bright and breezy, has a story a minute, and shows great familiarity with the Almighty. Some styles of music and singing may hold the attention with the throb of the music or the use of the voice. At best they can convey only aspects of the good news. No-one can communicate truly about genuine conviction of sin, or God as holy, or judgment, in a slick, bouncy, effervescent manner. Even if what he says or sings is true, he obscures the truth by the impression he creates. The medium belies the message. To paint only the brighter colours is exciting at first, but makes the total picture flat and insipid. With no depth of colour or contrast, even the bright colours lose their glory. The gospel's splendour disappears.

Wrong way round

Christians have been suffering too long from putting things the wrong way round in evangelism. We have *first* adopted various up-to-the-minute methods of communication and *then* allowed them to determine what kind of message we could get across. Rather, we need to start with the great truths of justification and then ask : what methods will make clear these truths of justification in all their glory and wholeness, their seriousness and joy?

We can see this from another angle. Justification is God's answer to a particular question. Ask the wrong question and God's answer will seem irrelevant. Ask first, 'How may I get fulfilment and purpose?' and justification may seem an involved, tortuous, academic answer. Ask first, 'What about my joy and happiness?' and it will seem a gloomy, even depressing, reply. But ask first about God, about eternity and hell, about sin and death – and justification will appear a radiantly clear, beautifully simple answer. A full and total answer. A humbling and uplifting answer. *God's* answer, bringing 'an inexpressible and glorious joy' (1 Pet. 1 :8).

Asking questions

Now everybody asks questions. Many enquire about religion and some ask about Christianity, yet few ask the right questions. In our evangelism we must seek to lead people to ask these. We must lead them from secondary or misguided queries to the primary issues. To do this, we must meet and speak to people where they are. We must also constantly be thinking, breathing and speaking the truths of justification. The test of our methods is : do they make justification clear?

Only if they do will they honour God and give lasting hope to those who hear.

Justification is crucial for evangelism, for without it there is no gospel. It is the only message that faces people with the vital issues. This is why it is crucial for each individual. Apart from justification, no-one has access to God, no-one has pardon or peace or adoption. Apart from justification by grace alone through faith alone, no-one is a Christian.

All other considerations about our standing with God are subordinate or irrelevant. A person may have had a Christian home. He may have had some form of Christian initiation as an infant or an adult; he may have attended church, been confirmed, become a church member or taught in Sunday School; he may have been very active in youth or community work or his Christian Union. On their own, those factors leave him ultimately in the same relationship to God as someone who has no Christian background of any kind.

The one vital question is whether a person is acquitted and accepted by God. It is not enough for us merely to affirm what we have done, in such terms as 'I have decided to follow Jesus'. This is not to minimize the importance of our response, for we should of course be totally committed, our bodies presented as a living sacrifice (Rom. 12 :1). We should be decidedly 'for' Jesus and what we say about Him is vital. But what He says about us matters even more. The ultimate issue is not about my verdict on God, but His on me. It is not whether I say 'Lord, Lord' but whether He says *either* 'I never knew you. Away from me !' *or* 'Come, you who are blessed by my Father; take your inheritance' (Mt. 7 :22, 23; 25 :34, 41). Justification is the only ground for personal confidence and hope before God.

Appendix 1
Justification: a summary

1. Justification concerns our relationship with God : the relationship of a holy God with guilty rebels.

2. Justification is the verdict of God, the Judge, declaring us acquitted and accepted. It is God not reckoning our sins against us, but rather putting His own righteousness to our account and delivering us from condemnation.

3. Justification is on the basis not of what sinners have done or can do, but of what Christ did as their representative and substitute. In His life He gave perfect obedience to God, so that in His death He might pay the penalty for others' sin and make a perfect sacrifice for them.

4. God justifies sinners not because of anything about them, but purely and wholly because of His grace.

5. Justification comes into experience not by anything the individual does, but only through trusting Christ.

6. Justification brings peace with God and access to Him, and leads to adoption and ultimately glory.

7. The faith that justifies issues in a life which grows in Christlikeness and expresses itself in love and obedience.

8. Justification brings assurance of salvation and support in spiritual depression.

9. Justification undergirds the whole Christian life and helps in all its experiences and problems.

10. Justification is crucial for the life and worship of the church and for its task of evangelism.

Appendix 2
Roman Catholicism and the meaning of justification

The Reformation stressed the doctrine of justification and expounded it in a biblical way. This forced the Roman Catholic Church to consider and define its position on justification. Ever since that time Roman Catholic writers have viewed justification as being essentially an *inward* change. My italics pick this out in the series of quotations following.

The Council of Trent met after the first flush of the Reformation to set out Roman teaching against what it regarded as the new errors. In its sixth session (1546–7) it said : 'Justification is not only the remission of sins, but *sanctification and renovation of the interior man* . . . whereby a man *becomes* just instead of unjust' (chapter 7).

John Henry Newman began as an Anglican, became a leading figure in the high church Oxford Movement of the 1830s, turned Roman Catholic and ended as a Cardinal. In his *Lectures on Justification* he wrote : justification comes 'through our sanctified wills and doings' (pp. 60f.). 'Man did not become guilty except by becoming sinful; he does not become innocent except by *becoming holy*' (p. 35). 'To "justify" *means* (these are Newman's italics) in itself "counting righteous", but includes *under* its meaning "making righteous"; in other words, the sense of the *term* is "counting righteous", and the sense of the *thing* denoted by it is "making righteous"' (p. 71). (And Newman pre-dated the famous dictum of Lewis Carroll's Humpty Dumpty : 'When *I* use a word, it means just what I choose it to mean, – neither more nor less.') It is hard to resist the conclusion that Newman knew what the words meant, but for his own reasons held another view and so imported the distinction between the 'term' and the 'thing signified'.

Again Newman makes his view clear : 'This is to be justi-fied, to receive the Divine Presence within us, and to be made a temple of the Holy Ghost' (p. 160). It is, of course, but a short step from this to the view that it is baptism which regenerates and so justifies. So Newman wrote : 'Faith jus-tifies, *because* baptism has justified' (p. 263). 'Baptism is expressly said to effect the first justification' (p. 260). 'Faith is the sole instrument (of justification) as preceded and made an instrument by the secret virtue of Baptism' (p. 261). To him, justification and renewal 'are convertible terms' (p. 98).

Many claim today that Trent and Newman represent only that version of Catholicism that existed up to the Second Vatican Council (1963–5). However, Vatican II does not renounce these older statements. It may be argued that it moves on from them in a more subtle way and that much of the ambiguity of the Council's language is designed to do just that. In fact Vatican II is hardly vocal at all on justifi-cation. The same views on justification have been in sub-stance expressed by leading Roman theologians in recent years. Hans Küng has written, for example : justification is 'a declaring of justice which *makes* just' (*Justification*, p. 206). God's work is 'the single act which simultaneously de-clares just and makes just' (p. 210). G. H. Tavard has writ-ten : justification '*makes* us just in complete reality' (*Pro-testantism*, p. 28). Louis Bouyer wrote : 'The *fiat* which saves must be a creative *fiat* : it causes what it enunciates, and makes us just in complete reality' (*The Spirit and Forms of Protestantism*, p. 28).

This is not just an idea within Roman Catholicism. Karl Barth, whom many liberal Protestants acclaimed as the leading theologian of the twentieth century, wrote that 'it is a declaring righteous which without any reserve can be called a *making* righteous . . . Man is not merely called righteous before God, but is righteous before God' (*Church Dogmatics*, Vol. IV, Part 1, p. 95). This same view appeals to Roman Catholic progressives since Vatican II. Writing of that Council, David F. Wells says that one 'important con-